A Cross Called Cancer

By
The Rev. Mark Moline

PRESS

Dedicated to my wife

Judy

Table of Contents

Prologue

"Then Jesus told his disciples, "If any want to become my followers, let them deny themselves and take up their cross and follow me." [1]

While not all that comforting, these sobering words do clarify the truth that sooner or later, his followers must each take up his own cross. For a good many in the near future, that cross will be a disease known as cancer. *"About 1,638,910 new cancer cases are expected to be diagnosed in 2012."* [2] Still, it was with significant reservation and much consternation that I subsequently entitled this work concerning my cross - my cancer. Why all of the concern about the title? Primarily, I wanted to avoid the extreme symbolic jargon that portrays both the cross and cancer as tantamount to death sentences. "The improved bench-mark cancer survival rate is now at *better than 67% for all Americans diagnosed with cancer between 2001 and 2007."* [3] Thus cancer is certainly no longer as lethal as it was in my youth forty and fifty years ago. Much progress has been made as this 2007 five-year survival figure cannot include the very latest treatments and technology. By its very numerical nature, it must lag five years behind. Still, we can expect continued improvement in the cancer survival rate during the next several years. There is hope!

Likewise, the cross was once considered a sure and certain tool of death but has now become the Christian believer's spiritual symbol of hope, the symbol of the death of death. Because of Christ's work on the cross, spiritual death no longer exists for the believer. We may be expected to suffer as others and eventually experience a biological death. But we believe that because Christ died there, we are spared that spiritual separation from God. We are spared the need to cry out, "My God, my God, why have you forsaken me?" We may have to take up a cross in this phase of life, but we need not die on it. We are alive for eternity because of God's love lived out through his suffering, and there-in rests the good news of faith in the Gospel.

A Cross Called Cancer was chosen for the book's title because its analogy reflects God's comforting love and presence in this mutual love, compassion, and suffering experienced by both God creator and humankind created. God suffered because of his love and compassion for us. "*God responded to this pain of ours in an astonishing way: he made it serve as testimony to his own pain. God could only reveal his pain to man through our own pain. God uses our pain as testimony to his. What happens to our pain? By serving as a witness to the pain of God, our pain is transformed into light; it becomes meaningful and fruitful.*"[4] The title of this book reflects that light, for it was in that light of suffering that I discovered that I did not serve a distant, uninvolved God. My God loves me enough to suffer with me. His loving presence means everything to me.

During the early stages of my own cancer diagnosis, I worried, wrestled with emotions, read, and prayed even as I knew I could only let go and wait for God's timing in this matter. "Faith in Love," and "faith and love" carried me through that difficult phase. I am thankful for my intellect, but I found it insufficient to reason my way through that ordeal. I needed to fight cancer with all my strength, but I didn't need to fight God over the question "why." My reasoning was no match for God's wisdom and love. I simply needed to have faith in a God who is love. I needed to believe. I needed to take up my cross and follow Him. My prayer became, 'Thy will be done!' Did I really have enough faith in God's love to truly believe that His will would be best for me? I needed to drink in and draw strength and patience from the love that, with such abundance, surrounded and embraced me.

Very few live a life free of suffering. Eventually, the time arrives for each of us to take up our cross of disease or traumatic injury. *"For everything there is a season, and a time for every matter **under heaven**."*[5] Cancer is certainly a matter under heaven, and thus my diagnosis brought on a season of suffering and healing. It was a season for me to take up my cross. There I sat with six to eight weeks to recuperate following my first of three major surgeries with only our blind dog 'Talbot' and my trusty word processor to keep me company during the day. I like to write, and I had a story to tell, thus I attempted to reduce to writing all that had taken place in the preceding few weeks. Because it was a story of both joy and suffering, I attempted to write ever so mindful of the prudent advice of Trappist Monk Thomas Merton, *"Suffer without imposing on others a theory of suffering, without weaving a new philosophy of life from your own material pain, without proclaiming yourself a martyr, without counting out the price of your courage, without disdaining sympathy and without seeking too much of it."*[6] I also undertook this writing because I desperately needed something to occupy my time. Talbot and I could only take so many walks in a day. I did want to keep my wife, children, friends, and acquaintances informed, to express heartfelt appreciation to them all, to sort out my thoughts, reactions, and reflections, and to try to discern some meaning and/or sense of order to all of this.

I must confess that the year 2005 did not proceed at all as I had originally planned. On Good Friday in the early spring, I celebrated my sixtieth birthday in what I thought was relative good health and was optimistic about my general physical well being. I was completely unaware of the massive tumor that overwhelmed my right kidney or the silent cancerous tumor growing in my colon. I felt great! Little did I know or even suspect the spiritual, emotional, and physical roller coaster that awaited me during the remainder of that year. That subsequent uncertain and wobbly emotional ride proved to be chaotic and left me searching for structured answers to personal questions. I think I already had many of the answers; perhaps I simply needed to sort them all out. Writing helped me do just that.

I come from a generation that was taught to diagram sentences. While some of the proper grammar didn't stick, that carefully structured dissection of the written word still haunts my thought process. Ideas, impressions, opinions, and reactions float around as thoughts, feelings, and musings. Like parts of speech, they are parts of life, and if I can just get them penned down on paper, then I can methodically dismember them. Once dismembered, they are ripe for the remembering, and it is in that careful reflective and arranged remembering that I often find their order and truth.

The chaotic ride began in late May when I was diagnosed with Renal Cell Carcinoma, and my primary care physician told me it didn't look good. He literally told me, *"You had better get your affairs in order."* My surgeon confirmed the RCC diagnosis even after surgery and the removal of my right kidney and the huge bleeding tumor that completely overwhelmed and obstructed it. The final pathology reports were due back seven to nine days following surgery. However, there was much delay as the tissue was tested and retested. The doctors didn't seem to trust the initial miraculous results. I don't think they appreciated the relevance of all the prayers being offered on my behalf. Twenty days following surgery, the doctors finally accepted the consistent results which placed me in a category of less than 3% of folks with kidney tumors presenting the characteristics of mine. The unwelcome cancer-like growth was Oncocytoma, a completely benign tumor. Once again, I felt great – for a season.

As summer faded into early autumn, I returned to work and put the finishing touches on my story. My three month CT Scan proved I was healthy and cancer free with my one remaining kidney and renal anatomy. However, my doctor informed me the CT Scan did not present the clearest picture of my colon and scheduled what was expected to be a routine colonoscopy. However, during that follow-up procedure, and to my great surprise and bitter disappointment, the examining doctor found a two-centimeter mass, and the needle biopsy indicated it was indeed cancer of the colon. So I really did have cancer after all.

The kidney tumor was truly benign, but this was a new primary tumor. The two tumors were in no manner linked or related. But in my emotional disappointment and frustration, I linked the two together as though they had been one cancer. Gone was God's glory in all of the answered prayer and claims of a miraculous healing. I was confused. Had it been cancer after all, and had it spread? How many more cancers were there yet undiscovered? I dutifully underwent my second major abdominal surgery and the top half of my colon was removed. This was followed by an even lengthier period of recuperation as I returned to my word processor. I once again started writing with far more questions than answers.

For a time, it seemed as though I would live out Ezekiel's warning of, *"Disaster after disaster! See it comes."*[7] But it didn't come, at least not in the form of total disaster. I encountered no great disaster even considering the emergency surgery required to combat the post-surgical infection that fought my body for weeks and weeks. That emergency operation was my third major abdominal surgery within five painful months. I actually spent thirty-eight days of one sixty-day period in the hospital to include five days in intensive care. More than three of those days were spent on life support in a coma. Post-surgical infections can be very nasty and sometimes fatal. With three major abdominal surgeries in five months, I began to really stagger and stumble under the weight of the cross I carried. However, with the skill of great physicians, the prayers of believers, the love of the best wife and children, I began to feel the real presence and strength of a loving, suffering God. He was close at hand. This is not to imply that I will never again face serious physical problems. An illness and trauma-free future is impossible for any of us to achieve this side of eternity. But for now, that wild and chaotic ride is finished, thanks to God's grace.

Long Live the King

~~~

Approximately 700 years before the time of Christ, there lived an interesting man by the name of Hezekiah. This man Hezekiah had his failings, faults, and weaknesses, but he very strongly believed in and served the God of Abraham, Moses, and David. With the assistance and counsel of his friend and spiritual advisor, Isaiah, he served as one of the few good Judahite kings of the Old Testament. Historically, he is considered a good king because of his very strong faith. During his reign, he destroyed false idols, reinstituted Mosaic Law, and generally turned the hearts of his subjects back to the God of Abraham.

King Hezekiah commissioned an engineering project that resulted in the digging of a 1,750-foot tunnel designed to help carry water from a spring in the Kidron Valley into the City of Jerusalem, where it emptied into the newly formed Pool of Siloam. Seven hundred years later, Christ sent a blind man to that pool to wash and thus gained his sight. He was miraculously healed. There is a subtle "healing" link here between the old and the new, for in the prime of Hezekiah's life and work, he was suddenly struck down by a deadly illness. He summoned Isaiah, who told him he had better get his affairs in order for he was going to die as a result of this illness. Isaiah's message was much the same as my doctor had given me.

Certain contemporary Christian authors and commenters have been critical of Hezekiah because of his apparent fear of death and love of this life. However, I would suggest that this is a fairly cheap shot to take from this side of the first Easter morn by scholars who have not experienced imminent, life-threatening illness. Unlike St. Paul of New Testament times, Hezekiah did not look forward to biological death with delight and great joy. Like me, and I suspect a lot of other more honest believers, he loved this life and was not prepared to die. Isaiah left him alone to die, and alone, he wept bitterly and prayed, petitioning God for healing. Isaiah soon returned to tell Hezekiah that God had seen him crying, heard his faithful plea, and decided to add 15 years to his time on earth. Hezekiah recovered and wrote poetry to reflect his healing encounter with God. In part, it reads:

"I said in the prime of my life,
must I enter the place of the dead?
Am I to be robbed of the rest of my years?
I said, never again will I see the Lord God
while still in the land of the living.
Never again will I see my friends
or be with those who live in this world.
My life has been blown away
like a shepherd's tent in a storm.
It has been cut short,
as when a weaver cuts cloth from a loom.
Suddenly, my life was over.

I waited patiently all night,
But I was torn apart as though by lions.
Delirious, I chattered like a swallow or a crane,
and then I moaned like a mourning dove.
My eyes grew tired of looking to heaven for help.
I am in trouble, Lord. Help me.

But what could I say?
For he himself sent this sickness.

Now I walk humbly throughout my years
because of this anguish I have felt.
Lord, your discipline is good,
for it leads to life and health.
You restore my health and allow me to live!
Yes, this anguish was good for me,
For you have rescued me from death;
And forgiven all my sins.
For the dead cannot praise you;
They can not raise their voices in praise.
Those who go down to the grave
can no longer hope in your faithfulness.
Only the living can praise you as I do today.
Each generation tells of your faithfulness to the next.
Think of it. The Lord is ready to heal me!
I will sing his praises with instruments
every day of my life
in the Temple of the Lord.[8]

My completely unanticipated and unforeseen diagnosis of kidney cancer quickly drew my attention to this Old Testament king whose reign was devoted to healing his sick kingdom. I found many parallels between the spiritual healing of his nation and people, his personal need for physical healing, and his ties to the subsequent healing ministry of Christ. I found, captured there in his poem, a spiritual and emotional process I myself initially lived through following my own disturbing diagnosis. I suspect others with similar experiences also commonly pass this way.

While seemingly contrived and somewhat distracting, I carved Hezekiah's healing poem into manageable perfunctory steps so that I could better understand just what was happening to me. These steps were not distinct, orderly, or sequential. That was an emotionally chaotic time, and thus these steps, which I so neatly arrange here, were actually experienced as real but vague, intermittent, and sometimes ambiguous. Nevertheless, I perceived them as follows.

1, Shock and Fear
2. Frustration and Disappointment
3. Loss and Loneliness
4. Anguish and Mental Suffering
5. Call for Help
6. Humility and Surrender
7. Faith and Rescue
8. Praise and God's Grace

Shock and Fear

"I said in the prime of my life, must I enter the place of the dead?"

I had been feeling fine. Some call cancer "the silent killer" because it often presents no symptoms or pain until the disease is advanced. Such was the case with me. I had experienced absolutely no previous symptoms when, at two or three A.M. one morning, I awoke with the feeling of a full bladder. Perhaps I am being a bit too graphic here, but I had to use the bathroom in the small hours of the morning, which is not at all unusual for a man sixty years of age. The moon was full that morning in suburban Atlanta, so I arose and stumbled half awake in the semi-darkness to the bathroom. The moonlight flooding through the second floor window was just bright enough for me to discern a mysterious hue of red gathering in the commode basin. I then flipped the light switch on and saw the toilet bowl was full of blood; my blood. Now I was awake! I was shocked. What was wrong with me? Was this a bad dream? I was alone, and I was scared.

Paul writes to the Corinthians, *"I want you to be free from anxieties."* How could I be anything but anxious? Don't worry! Of course, that is a lot easier said than done. In fact, I would suggest that for us to be literally free from all anxieties is next to impossible. I suspect that I would grow anxious merely trying to be anxiety free. I'm afraid I would probably fail in such an attempt. To some degree, I think in many of life's situations, a little worry is even a healthy thing. I suppose worry in and of itself is a normal human emotion. Worry is not involuntary sin. Excessive worry may be destructive and ought to be avoided. However, I think worry can be a lot like food. If you don't eat enough, you will become sick. At the same time, if you eat too much, you will become sick. You can eat yourself sick. You can certainly worry yourself sick. If you are worried that you worry too much, go see a mental health counselor. There are all sorts of devastating anxiety disorders, and I am not qualified to adequately address such in this writing.

By-and-large though, I firmly believe appropriate worry can keep us safe. Pilots seem to capture what I'm referring to here in one brief observation. You've heard it before, "There are old pilots and there are bold pilots, but there are no old, bold pilots." An appropriate degree of worry or concern can help keep us safe and healthy. I'm diabetic. I worry about my sugar level. That's a healthy worry for me to have. I was worried about blood in my urine and knew to go see a doctor as soon as possible.

It was a lot more than simple worry I experienced early that morning. I was frightened. A factor concerning worry seems to be "fear." Are fear and worry one and the same? Some say they can't be separated. They claim worry is fear, and fear is worry. I disagree. It may all be semantics or a question of degree. But if I tell you, "I'm worried that the battery in my Jeep is about to die, I just hope it starts today," such is worry. I'm not frightened by the fact that it won't start; I'm worried. I'm not afraid of the battery. On the other hand, if we're driving down a steep mountain road, and it's the worn brakes I'm worried about; now that is fear. Worry and fear are different – but there is a point when worry can become fear; like at the crest of that mountain road.

"Fear not!" That's one of the most frequently quoted

admonitions in all of Holy Scripture. I don't believe God wants his children frightened. But once again, this is easier said than done. I've never met a Christian believer who claimed to know no fear. If nothing else, let us strive to be honest and candid one with another. Let us confess the truth about our fears. God is not intimidated by our openness and honesty. After all, Christ said he was the "truth."

"Are you scared?" Now I always ask that pastoral question of my parishioners facing crises. I try to make it easy for them to be honest and admit that they are, if indeed they are. Openly acknowledging fear is the first step in healing fear. Are you afraid? I think I ask that question because fear was precisely my initial emotion to my personal health crisis. I was afraid of dying; I almost did. It was good for me to spiritually work through that fear. I was scared, and yet, my faith was stronger than ever. I wasn't afraid of going to heaven, I wasn't afraid of facing Christ. I was afraid of biological death. There are worse things than fear of biological death, like fearing death and not being able to admit it to others. That combination leaves us both frightened and alone. There is no shame in being frightened.

While fear is not God's will for the believer, the spiritual process of overcoming fear is just that. Overcoming fear with God's help is, in and of itself, a divine miracle. I think God wants to be involved in our fears. Like a loving parent assuring a frightened child, God wants to be there to comfort us. God knows we will be frightened, and I think God wants to save us from unbearable fear. We read a most hauntingly beautiful and power-filled passage from Romans, "*The Spirit helps us in our weakness. We do not know what we ought to pray for, but the spirit itself intercedes for us with groans that words can-not express. And he who searches our hearts knows the mind of the Spirit, because the Spirit intercedes for us in accordance with God's will. And we know that in all things – in all things – God works for the good of those who love him, who have been called according to his purpose.*"[9]

Fear is terrible, and yet the process for overcoming fear is restorative. That process is prayer, love, faith, and community. *"Do not worry about anything, but in everything by prayer and supplication with thanksgiving let your requests be made known to God And the Peace of God, which surpasses all understanding, will guard your hearts and your minds in Christ Jesus."*[10]

God's peace is there for us even in the midst of our fears of death. So often folks use or hear a colloquial phrase like, "prepare to meet your maker," and they will associate that with death. In reality, meeting God has everything to do with life and nothing at all to do with the dying process. Again, fear of death is not a very proper introduction to Christ. Meeting Christ face-to-face is not about death; that meeting is all about life. Spiritual rebirth is birth; it is not death. Spiritual salvation is not about death; it is about life after death. Life after death is life, not death. I was prepared to 'meet my maker,' I just wasn't ready to die. This side of the cross, can I draw strength and reality from both Hezekiah and St. Paul? My biological death may be the gateway to eternal life, but it is solely part of this temporal life. By its very nature, eternity knows no death.

Our natural death may be the gateway to eternity, but now I envision it more as the back gate leading from this life rather than the front door of paradise. I am in no way suggesting here the feasibility of purgatory or some intermediate state. This may all be a matter of phraseology and mental image, but I no longer find it particularly helpful to relate biological death so closely to eternal spiritual life. They are two very separate entities. They are close, but very different. Death is a part of this journey. It is sequestered in time. For me, it now belongs to the future. Someday it will occupy my now, but never the "eternal now" that is paradise. Neither will it take its place in the past, for then time will be no more.

My own principal mental image of death and eternal life is somewhat like that of a bad dream in its relationship with the bright morning thereafter. I have seldom experienced vivid dreams. However, when I was eight or nine years of age, I remember going through a short phase when I had frequent nightmares. I have not the slightest idea as to their cause, and they presented no common theme and very little continuity. Then after just a few months, they simply went away or ceased to occur. But I can remember dreading to go to sleep at night because I knew I would encounter all sorts of terribly frightening circumstances in my dreams. But come morning, the rising sun would break in through my bedroom window, and the new morning would always chase away the fear and pain.

Something seems to be intrinsically wrong with so closely linking biological death with eternity. The two seem so inconsistent and conflicting. Of course, in our current human condition, we can't have one without the other. However, I think some well-meaning believers do attempt to meld the two too closely together. They fuse these two opposites in their evangelism and their faith. My mother used to tell a relevant true story from her many years in a fundamentalist evangelical church. It was the type of church that routinely required personal public testimonies from its members during worship. Each week, the members were expected to stand up and "witness" to everyone about the wonderful things God was doing in their lives. There was one elderly lady who always gave the very same testimony each week; "I'm just living for the day I can go home to heaven to be with Jesus. That's my heart's desire. I'm looking forward to heaven to be with my Master."

One week, the woman's husband installed a new gas stove, and being quite elderly himself, he apparently made a few crucial errors in its installation. They turned it on and literally blew up the house, but both miraculously escaped relatively unscathed. The following Sunday, the little congregation braced themselves as the wife stood to testify. To everyone's great surprise, she didn't even flinch as she proclaimed how blessed she was just to be there that Sunday morning in their midst. She talked about how God had miraculously spared her from death and certain destruction. Apparently, it had taken that violent explosion to blast apart the joys of eternity from the fearful tragedy of a painful biological death.

James Boswell asked Samuel Johnson if fear of death wasn't natural to man. Johnson replied, *"So much so that the whole of life is but keeping away the thoughts of it."*[11] I think Johnson was being brutally honest here, and yet we, as modern and post-modern Christian believers, tend to collectively deny that natural apprehension. We often mask that apprehension and fear with feigned courage in an attempt to strengthen our own faith and that of others. We fear that our fear of dying will betray a lack of faith for we know that in John's Gospel Christ decreed, *"Peace I leave with you; my peace I give to you. I do not give to you as the world gives. Do not let your hearts be troubled, and do not let them be afraid."*[12] Don't let yourself be afraid! Jesus spoke of troubled and frightened hearts, and so I suspect he was addressing spiritual fear of death, while Johnson was simply confronting emotional fear of dying. There is a colossal difference and distance between spiritual fear of spiritual death and emotional fear of biological death. Our faith is not pre-programmed to dispel that emotional fear of biological death, and we shouldn't pretend it is.

Too many preachers have attempted to label all fear as the opposite of faith. It is not. Doubt is the opposite of faith. One may have very strong faith and still experience ordinary human fear. Fear is a common and sometimes, to some degree, a healthy emotion. In fact, when recognized, confessed to God, controlled, and managed with care, fear can serve as both a strong motivator of courage and an excellent tool for survival. Confessed fear serves as an invitation for God's intervention. I'm sure it is true that fear, unchecked by faith, may grow to become spiritually debilitating. I think Christ dreaded the cross but had sufficient faith in the Father to embrace that which he dreaded.

The Psalmist proclaims, *"Even though I walk through the valley of the shadow of death, I will fear no evil, for you are with me."*[13] I would suggest this line refers to fear of evil, not fear of death. In this life, we travel through a valley that has its spiritual evils. But because the Good Shepherd walks beside us, carrying his staff that now resembles a Roman cross, we need fear no evil. Because of that cross, death is no longer a spiritual evil for the believer. It is just a shadow, not a full eclipse. And yet, even without its sting, it still casts a large and ominous shadow across our valley. Even as a defeated, powerless enemy, it stands looming there between us and the sun and presents each of us with something that we must physically and emotionally pass through to get to the full light.

We don't see death; we only see its big, ugly, painful shadow, and we are frightened. That emotion is quite natural and in no way should such be interpreted as a lack of faith and trust in the Shepherd that accompanies us. If anything, it makes us walk a little closer to the Shepherd and thus trust him and his cross even more. The Shepherd does not want his sheep frightened but does not require them to be fearless. He knows they are sometimes frightened. He is the fearless one, and as we walk that valley, he leans over and whispers in our ear, *"All authority in heaven and on earth has been given to me."*[14] Quite simply put, he wants us to trust him.

Jesus explained that he wasn't giving peace as the world gives. We know the world gives us the worthy, but relatively shallow, concept of mind-over-matter. But Christ promises spirit over matter. Again, there is an intrinsic difference. The

23

mind is of and from and dependent upon the body, while the spirit transcends the limits of our biological self. We find great courage and peace in Christ's promise of spiritual immortality, and yet we ignore the possibility that there probably is a subtle, and often denied, but widespread dread amongst even the believers that they must someday experience a biological death. Our faith in ultimate victory and eternal life may be very strong indeed, but still our human predicament confronts us. Again, that fear is to be expected and should be viewed as a reality of life rather than a sign of weakness or lack of faith or spiritual courage.

One cancer information web site currently advertises under the catchphrase, '*Fight fear with knowledge.*' One would indeed be foolish to in anyway discourage the procurement of knowledge. We all should become more knowledgeable of this dreadful disease. In fact, knowledge is a crucial weapon in the war against cancer. However, we must be honest enough to recognize knowledge as being a very subjective weapon in battling individual and personal fear. Its effectiveness against fear is completely subjective. I tried it, and it didn't work for me. The knowledge was valuable in many ways but quite counterproductive in waylaying my fears.

I visited the library and found much encouragement about the treatment of cancer in general. Survival rates and even cures are far better today than even a few years ago. However, the extent of encouragement the knowledge produced seemed to depend greatly upon the type and stage of cancer concerned. I found the five-year survival rate for large kidney tumors to be far lower than I had suspected, or even feared, in my ignorance. In fact, in all of those books and sources, I couldn't find any information about Renal Cell Carcinoma that encouraged me. I was better informed, and that is a good thing, but the knowledge just added to my fears. I left the library more frightened than when I arrived. Still, I was better off knowing just what confronted me.

Knowledge alone may not waylay the fears of a person suffering the advance stages of Renal Cell Carcinoma, while the person suffering the early stages of Colon Cancer will find increased knowledge quite encouraging. As beneficial as knowledge is, it may or may not be helpful in the fight against fear. Hope, faith, love, community, prayer, trust, honesty, and reasoned confrontation of fear, and the freedom to be afraid and show our fears are all good weapons we have in our arsenal against fear. However, superficial denial of fear will only add to the pain, disillusionment, and loneliness.

I've personally given up on the cultural standard that "grown men don't cry." Perhaps dying would be a little less frightening if we were allowed the freedom to be our emotional selves. I think we actually compound the pain of dying by insisting upon a denial of emotions. Hezekiah remained a mighty King and a spiritual hero of the faith even though he cried in the face of death. In the Garden of Gethsemane, The Messiah faced ominous death. Scripture tells us he was deeply grieved and threw himself on the ground. He then told his followers, *"the spirit is willing, but the flesh is weak."*[15] Great spiritual courage does not preclude emotional fear.

Frustration and Disappointment

*"Am I to be robbed of the rest of my years?
Never again will I see the Lord God while still
in the land of the living."*

I promptly visited my primary care physician the day following my frightening early morning symptoms. He told me, "This could be serious. I am sending you to an urologist." The receptionist gave me a name and phone number, and I called as soon as I returned home. The voice on the phone told me that the specialist was triple-booked, and it would be quite difficult to squeeze my visit into his busy schedule. But then my primary care physician's office-staff worked with them, and they managed to find a slot for me. I was squeezed into an over-booked urologist's schedule, and I felt squeezed. I am blessed with good health insurance and am not accustomed to standing in long lines, awaiting medical care. But on the day of my appointment, there was quite literally standing room only in his office reception area. I was annoyed. I was frustrated. That crowd and the long line of cubicle-like exam rooms gave me that familiar 'Henry Ford Assembly-line' feeling that we now find in many doctors' offices.

Henry Ford knew how to make automobiles, and he also knew how to make money. He mastered production efficiency. With some exceptions, that latter Henry Ford skill is one commonly shared by today's medical profession. I found it curious that my primary care physician has both a MD and a MBA. However, in all honesty, he is one who does not apply an assembly line approach to his practice. He always seems to take the time to talk to his patient as an individual. Perhaps he knows more than others that he is working on the customer, not the customer's car. So, he was wise, cautious, caring, and concerned enough about this customer to refer me to a specialist. That's just good business, and no doubt there is a legitimate business side to healing. I just think greed and healing make for lousy business partners, and oftentimes, the perceptions of the difference between "over-aggressive" and "necessary but sound" business practices blur for me, and I suspect for other patients. When our life is hanging in the balance, we all want the best, and we want special treatment. However, it just stands to reason that not everyone who expects such will find it.

I was eventually seated in Examining Room #2 of the urologist's office three days after my one and only experience with blood in my urine. When the doctor completed his Room #1 stopover, he came to #2 and me. It took him about fifteen minutes to perform some routine nomenclature checks and found everything to be 'OK'. He then simply said, "With blood in the urine, we are always concerned about cancer in the bladder and/or kidneys." I didn't like to hear that word *cancer*; it scared me. It seemed 'out-of-place' in relationship to my health issues. Others had cancer, not me. It didn't run in my family. None of my blood-relatives had ever been diagnosed with cancer. Thus, I assumed a strange emotive mixture of denial and arrogance. It initially served me well as an emotional defense system, but ultimately fed my frustration.

I initially assumed the additional test the doctor insisted upon would show my kidneys free of any cancer. I beat back my worst fears in a shallow and superficial hope and denial. However, I must have been mildly concerned as I said a short and cursory prayer asking God to make sure I didn't have cancer. "Give me something else that's easy to fix." That brief prayer coming in the midst of my arrogance was little more than a conjured-up spiritual insurance mini-policy.

As an Episcopal Priest, I do a lot of praying, and in those pre-diagnosis days, some were merely perfunctory "drive-by" prayers. I guess I too am capable of using an assembly-line approach in my work; perhaps that assembly line mentality has become more of a universally accepted approach to our lives than I once understood. Still, I considered this whole "passing blood thing" a fearful and troublesome disruption to my own overbooked schedule. I had cancer sufferers in need of counseling, prayer, my presence, and love. I resented the disruption of my own physical problems and found it all most frustrating. I had better things to do with my time than to hang out in doctor's offices. Surely it was some sort of minor virus or infection that would just go away. Perhaps the doctor could give me something for it. He did ask me about pain or discomfort in either bladder or kidney areas, and I told him that I had no other symptoms and that I felt great. He then scheduled what is commonly referred to as a 'CT Scan.' In my uninformed layman's terms, the 'CT Scan' just seemed to be an extensive series of x-rays of my kidneys. I know they were very good "x-rays," though, because the insurance bill for that one set of "pictures" was in excess of $4,000.

The initial urology office visit was on a Wednesday, and the following Wednesday, I still had not heard back from the doctor. I took that to be a good sign; surely if it were serious, they would contact me right away. I was doing some administrative work at the church when the urologist him-self finally called me. Obviously, I couldn't tell over the phone if he was between room #1 & #2 or if he had just finished some higher numbered cubicle, but as with my one previous contact, he seemed very proficient but hurried. I sensed that I was but one of several calls he had to make. He established that it was me on the other end of the line, and abruptly stated, "Your CT scan came back, and you have a large tumor on your right kidney, and that kidney will have to come out. You will have to come back in for some other tests; I want to take a look in your bladder. Do you have any questions?" It was just that abrupt, brief, and curt.

The thirty years prior to my seminary training were experienced as a police officer, and I had on different occasions had the wind physically knocked out of me. The good doctor's abrupt telephone words that day had the very same affect, and I couldn't believe I was hearing my own voice say, "No, I can think of no questions." The operative word there was "think." I couldn't think. I knew the doctor was in a hurry, and thus I had to be in a hurry. Of course I had questions, hundreds of questions, maybe even thousands of questions. It is not very self-flattering for a pastor who believes in and proclaims eternal life to admit, but my first question would have been, "How long do I have to live?"

The psalmist beseeches God, *"Teach us to number our days aright, that we may gain a heart of wisdom."*[16] How many days do we have? I think most of us ask ourselves and our God this question from the time when we first become aware of our own mortality. We would like to know, and yet we wouldn't want to know even if we could. Knowing the specific day of our demise, or possessing that "heart of wisdom," would give us more control and help us effectively manage our affairs and service to others and God. However, I suspect the temptation for manipulation would then be great and would probably be a detriment to our relationship with the Creator. God knows; we don't know, and that serves to remind us that God is the one in control.

I suspect that knowing the specific number of our days would cast a pall over this life. When this life is going well, it is quite enjoyable and exciting to get so caught up in our physical existence that we forget our temporary nature here on earth. We grow wary of traveling and like to act as though we have arrived. Nothing, though, will snap us out of that comfortable complacency quite like a stark road sign that tells us we are only a few miles from the end of our pilgrimage. The doctor's phone call that day was such a road sign, and it warned me that I was nearing my ultimate destination. That sign snapped me out of my comfort and complacency and left me feeling very temporary indeed.

How long do I have? *"Are we almost there, Daddy?"* That may be a good question for God, but a far better question for my doctor at that time would have been, "You are going to remove my right kidney, is the left one healthy and functioning well?" I knew people lived active lives with just one kidney, but as a diabetic, I wasn't sure my other kidney was OK. That urologist looked at a clear picture of what at least appeared to be a perfectly healthy left kidney. I'm sure that image didn't tell everything, but then, I wasn't looking for a premature ironclad guarantee, just a tiny scrap of hope. Perhaps he feared the worst and didn't want to risk giving me false hope.

Then I heard a young woman's voice on the line telling me she would set up an appointment for me and explained that the soonest she could squeeze me in would be the following Wednesday. There was that 'squeeze play' again. I had regained just enough breath to politely protest, "I think the doctor wants to see me earlier than a week from now." She replied, "Just a second," and was back with me in a few moments. "No, the doctor says Wednesday will do fine." Thus I simultaneously started out on both the seven worst days of my sixty-year life and the seven best days of my life.

I knew God would be there for me. I trusted my wife and children to stand by me through the worst. I am blessed with so many good friends who I knew would not abandon me. I turned to the Great Physician for comfort, and I turned to the library and to the Internet for information. I turned to family and good friends for both. I soon learned that regardless of their size, more than 90% of all tumors in the kidneys are cancerous. I learned that some are very fast acting, and I subsequently learned that more than 97% of all tumors characteristic with the images on my 'CT Scan' are **cancer**. I didn't like that word, and I really didn't care for those odds. I was scared. I had a miserable sick sinking feeling deep in my insides. I tried to force my mind to run ahead of my emotions but failed as fear, frustration, and disappointment overtook me. Real desperation gripped me.

I then found that cancer of the kidney is incurable if the cancer has metastasized. I soon added 'metastasized' to my rapidly growing list of disliked, scary words. The doctor had said it was large. Did large mean 'metastasized?' He wanted to look in my bladder; did it appear to have spread to the bladder? Again, the doctor was looking at those images and could have told me that there are no guarantees, but the tumor at least appeared to be restricted to the kidney, and the film gave no indication that the tumor had metastasized. I know he has competently handled these same circumstances many times before and doubtlessly has learned through experience the best approach to use. And then, too, perhaps he didn't want to get my hopes up only to have them dashed later. He knows better than I, but it seems to me even a trace of hope would have helped me accept the reality of it all. My frustration and fear reminded me of C.S. Lewis' observation that the man caught driving on a mountain road in a blizzard may need a view of the next three feet more than he needs the greater distant view.[17]

In retrospect, I was not so frustrated by the truth as I was by not knowing the truth or where and how to find it. I knew I faced major surgery and the removal of a kidney. I was mildly surprised at how quickly and easily I understood and adjusted to that news. It had to be done, that was now a given, and I simply wanted to get on with it. However, in this information age, the doctor expected me to wait another seven days, knowing he had the answers about my life and my prospects for the future, but he would be unable to share that with me sooner, I suspect, because he was over-booked. Perhaps I am too impatient and/or just expect too much, but I desperately needed relevant information, and I needed some assurance that someone with some medical expertise was in my corner. I just wanted a doctor who would take the time to sit with me and explain in detail what was going on in my body. It was initially both frustrating and disappointing to place my life and future into the hands of the medical profession. It seemed to me that this process was super efficient, systemic, and self-serving in that it was primarily concerned with that system rather than the patient. *"They have treated the wound of my people carelessly, saying peace, peace, when there is no peace."*[18] I felt like an unwelcome intruder into something far bigger than me and my meager concerns. After all, I was only the patient and not a very patient one at that.

Twentieth century theologian Kosuke Koyama likens such efficiency and bureaucracy to idolatry. He writes, *"Efficiency is suffocating meaning."* *"When the human environment is thus technologized, the uniqueness of the person will eventually suffer, and there may appear a faceless mass of people. The crucified Christ challenges such a technologically efficient way of dealing with people. Technology must serve the maintenance and development of human values, the values of sincerity and reliability in the human community."*[19]

Since those early encounters with an efficient and bureaucratic medical profession, I have also found that physicians have learned the hard way that it is simply litigiously safer to avoid sharing unsubstantiated possibilities, and even probabilities, in the mere interest of offering hope and peace of mind. Patients and their attorneys who file frivolous and greedy law suits need to know that they are hurting a good many innocent people far beyond the medical profession. That two million dollar jury award is nice for the attorneys, and I guess somewhat or somehow satisfying for the sufferer, but drags the rest of us down in far more than mere financial terms. The quality of our care suffers. Self-righteous jurors who award excessive punitive damages need to reflect upon the far-reaching, hurtful impact of the injustice they so irresponsibly mete out. Our physicians must be freed to prescribe hope.

My family and I lived in rural North Dakota in the early eighties, which was somewhat similar to living in the fifties just about anywhere else. It was wonderful up there, except for the long winters and terribly cold temperatures. We attended church with our family physician, and when we went in for an appointment, we would go into his office, and he would sit down behind his big wooden desk in business attire. We usually began the visit with an informal discussion which greatly put us at ease and gave the doctor a good understanding of our general state of mind and body. Then he would stand up, start to don his white coat, and say, 'Let's go in and examine you." It was nothing less than a healing ritual that resulted in individual comfort and care.

The office nurse would then escort us into the examining room, prepare us for the examination, and the doctor would then enter to do the clinical work. Then we would all return to his office for the follow-up consultation. It was always reassuring, ritualistic, and quite reminiscent of by-gone days. I suppose this all could be viewed as really little more than an extension of the "placebo effect," but it was comforting and gave one the sense of being in the midst of a caring community. It tended to put patient and doctor on the same team. Now that's all gone by-the-by, but still I would not trade all the advances made in health care since for those days when that compassionate healing ritual was a common practice. However, I fail to understand why efficiency must cancel out personal attention and care. I simply question why we can't have both. Again, I guess I just want too much, and that leads to frustration-a common frustration that many cancer patients share.

The commonly applied assembly-line approach takes its toll in stress, estrangement, and lost peace of mind. It presents veiled natural fallout that hustles the patient toward the exit door. The doctors seem to be in a hurry, the nurses and staff also seem to be in a hurry; how dare one slow patient be the weak and unskilled player on this highly efficient team? Cautious information gathering takes valuable time away from the group effort. This residual team impatience often leaves the sufferer headed for the parking lot, inadequately aware of his or her condition and feeling powerless in the face of awesome ambiguity.

Combine this process with the tormented stress of seemingly endless waiting for long delayed test results, and one finds him or herself dealing with the chaos of a very frustrating 'hurry up and wait' mentality. At least that is the impact it had on me, not knowing what to pray for or just how I should pray. My frustrated craving for solid and specific information ballooned out of proper proportion to overshadow my prayer life. I was simply too alarmed to realize that God could have cared less how I phrased my prayers. God didn't need me to explain the details; he only wanted me to turn to him and to trust in him.

How should I pray and what should I tell others? Friends and family had questions that I couldn't answer. For some unknown reason, I felt like I personally owed others an explanation. It was as though I had to produce. I think perhaps I felt out of control. I was miserable being kept uninformed, being kept in the dark. Many cancer survivors have told me this hurried suspenseful waiting is common and can be the worse part of the whole ordeal. In fact, my seven-day wait pales in comparison to others' stories of waiting for doctors and test results.

Treatment centers are aware of the painful time delays in obtaining quality test results upon which they can accurately determine the type and extent of treatment required. Jonathan Simons, director of the Winship Cancer Institute at Emory University, recently expressed hope for a better day. *"One day, you're going to get a biopsy, and at the end of the day, we'll be able to tell you how long we'll have to treat you and exactly how we will do it. We'll be able to take every person's cancer and personalize it."*[20] How refreshing and hopeful it is to hear someone from within the health care profession championing this concept of personalizing disease. I think that is what I wanted and maybe even selfishly and/or naively expected. It only makes sense for the treatment to be as unique as the individual and his or her cancer. But, while the medical profession has come a long way in the past few years, it is still simply a work in progress. Perhaps we do expect too much too soon. Of course, the obvious and natural result is frustration and disappointment.

The institutionalized medical, legal, and other social service systems are at times bound to frustrate and disappoint the individual who suffers and struggles with cancer. They are systems, not communities; organizational structures, not people. Yes, there are individual care-givers working within these systems that will consistently treat you with individualized loving care. They will even prioritize your comfort over their own. Thank God for such angels of mercy. However, they must always function within parameters established by commissions, committees, boards, and sometimes shareholders. Such decision making bodies must prioritize the survival and efficiency of the institution and its mission over your personalized care. They can, and most do, try to balance the needs of the individual with the needs of the institution; but the result is a well intentioned balancing act rather than a perfect science. Thus there are unavoidable frustrations. The individual sufferer is left with a choice of simply enduring or countering these frustrations. Of course, it is most counter-productive to fight the system that is trying to provide you with care. Such frustrations must be countered with the sufferer's own faith, friends, and family, for they are true community.

Loss and Loneliness

"Never again will I see my friends or be with those who live in this world."

As I type this account, 'Talbot' sits on the floor beside my chair watching me pound away at these keys, and then I realize Talbot isn't watching anything. He is a blind dog. He hears the keys of the word processor. The vet explained that from birth he has had no blood supply to his retinas. No pool of Siloam for poor Talbot. Ironically, Judy and I selected him from among hundreds of dogs at the county animal shelter because of his great eye contact. We thought we knew from past experience that we could tell a lot about a dog just by his eyes.

Talbot was cute and had very intelligent-looking eyes. They seemed so clear. He wagged his tail and watched our every move as we walked down the long row of well-lit kennels. But 'Talbot' was in the dark; he hadn't 'seen' anything in five years of life. He heard us walking and talking; he smelled us and then touched us. He very confidently compensates for his blindness by relying upon his other senses and trusting in those senses. He is a great little con-artist; so good, in fact, that the folks who work at the shelter didn't even know he was blind. Of course, he doesn't know he is blind. Neither did we, until we got him home when he ran nose-first into a couple of walls and a tree he encountered in that unfamiliar territory. And so Talbot's perseverance and courage jolts me into the realization that my original fear of the unknown was not all that bad for me after all. While I didn't realize it at the time, being kept in the dark by the doctor's busy schedule compelled me to compensate for my informational blindness by placing more trust and faith in God, family, and friends.

Only in very recent times have our care providers just begun to appreciate, and to some extent understand, the role animals can play in the care, treatment, and nurture of those of us suffering life threatening illness. The love and companionship of one of God's creatures serves as a constant reminder of life and its source. Talbot is blind, not deaf, so I had someone to talk to during those long daytime hours when I was eventually left home to recuperate on my own. His companionship was precious. Just how much he understands remains unknown for certain. I suspect he understands more than most will accept. But still he could hear, and I could do enough understanding for both of us. Also, he seems to live for the here and now with little or no concept of future or past; that serves as a much-needed example for me. He lives for the here and now. Thus he makes the most of each new day living his doggie life to the fullest.

Talbot the blind dog loves to run, and we let him when it's safe; that is, at the beach or in a big grassy field. He finds it quite difficult to wait for me once he senses that it is safe. Once off the leash, he will simply run around and around in big repetitious circles until I can catch him, and catching him is quite easy. You just walk up to the edge of his circle and grab him when he comes around again. He knows better than to strike out on his own across unfamiliar ground lest he run head-on into a fence, a wall, or even a raised curb. He is too impatient to wait for me and yet too blind to go for his own walk, so he ultimately finds himself simply running in circles.

I'm a lot like Talbot. When I was first diagnosed with Renal Cell Carcinoma, I wanted to strike out on my own. I trusted God, and I was certainly willing to work with doctors and other medical care givers, but I wanted to manage my own mental and emotional response to this new and unwelcomed direction my life was taking. I didn't want to drag my family and friends into my misery. Then too, I sensed I was losing control over my future and wanted to do things my way as long as I was physically able. I didn't want others slowing me down in my personal process of adjustment to a serious illness. I'm often just too impatient to wait even for God, much less my friends and family.

Yet to this day, I still don't understand that initial feeling of impatience in the face of illness. Perhaps I was just too emotionally blind to see that I wasn't equipped to take my own walk through that time of suffering. I didn't realize I couldn't do it on my own. Consequently, I initially found myself running in lonely, self-centered emotional circles. I feel like God walked up to the edge of my running circle, waited for me to come back around, and then reached out and grabbed me in tender love.

My wife and I celebrated our wedding anniversary three weeks following my subsequent surgery to remove my right kidney and the tumor. Thirty-nine years earlier, we committed to love one another "for better or for worse, in sickness and in health," and that summer, we discovered just what all that really means. I will never again perform a wedding and use that line without thinking of Judy's love for me. Judy has never been a passive little woman. She is strong. She has always been strong and courageous, and she was the stoic epitome of spousal steadfastness and devotion throughout this entire ordeal. I know it wasn't easy for her, but she was always there for me and never once let her anguish show. As such, she was a loving source of strength and confidence when I needed her most.

Judy's faith in God is very strong indeed! I gave her the initial bad news as we sat together in a parking lot. I was picking her up following a hair salon appointment, and the startling news that I would lose one of my kidneys only prompted her to pray a prayer of great trust and confidence. She reassured me that, "with God's help, we would get through whatever comes our way." She smiled and hugged me, and that did a lot for my faith. Even in the face of evidence to the contrary, she never once conceded that my illness would even detract from my ministry. From the very first, she asserted that God was using all of this as a positive "wake-up call" for both of us. Her joy was intact. Some might consider her stoicism as little more than emotional denial, but they would be wrong, for she was right all along. Her calm faith is contagious.

Then, too, I now realize that parents of young children really need to catalogue somewhere in the recesses of their minds the image of their children parenting them someday. I can remember my small children on occasion being frightened and/or hurting and coming to me for solace. Those were precious moments indeed, but I never imagined the tables would turn so quickly. My daughter dropped her busy work schedule in Los Angeles and purchased an airline ticket for Atlanta just to be there with me when the doctor was scheduled to review the CT Scan images with me for the first time. She knew that if the results were negative, that could be a difficult time for me; she knew I could be frightened and hurting, and she wanted to be there for me. Both my adult son and daughter were there for Judy and me during and after the surgery. As I lie in my hospital bed looking up at my wife, my son, and my daughter, I realized that all of those precious moments from years ago were far more than good memories. They were nothing less than a direct reflection of God's love at work in our lives.

I suspect there is a tendency to cast our families in their very best light as we reflect upon just how precious they are to us during times of pain and suffering. This is okay, as we should be proud of them and the role they play in our troubled needs. However, in doing so, we can make our families appear perfect and flawless to others, and there is possible negative fallout from this pride. That is, others may feel their families are not up to the task. They know their families to be less than perfect and may worry that their loved ones already have too many problems to cope with the additional stress cancer can bring into a family.

When I was a child, I used to watch a television show called "Ozzie & Harriet." The Nelsons were always happy, they always wore nice clothes, they lived in a beautiful house on a beautiful street in a beautiful neighborhood; they were never sick or tired or lonely or angry. Rickie and David didn't fight like my brothers and I did. That family smiled a lot more than my family did, and everyone was always treated fairly, and they never needed for anything. I can remember naively thinking, "Now that's the way a family is supposed to be." I was just a young child, television was brand new, and I didn't know any better, but that was just a TV show; it was not real life. In real life, all families have problems.

Today, a rather significant segment of the church at large finds itself caught up in extolling "American Family Values." As worthy as that campaign may be, care must be taken to insure that we are celebrating biblical "Christian Family Values" rather than an American cultural "Ozzie and Harriet" mindset. Our Bible is not a book of fairy tales, it is a book of truth, and the truth is families have problems. By fairy tale standards, we find no perfect families in the Bible. In fact, I find a persistent theme of family trouble throughout Holy Scripture. It's almost overwhelming; that is, until we see the biblical focus is upon the healing, recovery, and restoration of injured families.

Obviously, the whole idea of 'family' gets off to a really poor start with two brothers named Cain and Abel. You know that unhappy story. Then there is Noah's family. After they survived the flood, Noah went on a drinking binge and caused all sorts of very ugly problems for his family, but then we seldom read that story past the rainbow. In real life, somewhere over the rainbow can be a family disappointment, as Noah's family discovered.

Jacob seemed like a good dad, but he played favorites with his children. He loved Joseph more than his other sons. This quite naturally hurt the others and caused them to hate Joseph. King David was not a good husband. He caused and experienced some terrible family problems. He made a lot of mistakes as a husband and as a Father, and Absalom was neither a good son nor a good brother. The list of dysfunctional families in the Bible seems endless. Then a perfect God stepped into human history. And wouldn't you just know; he did so as part of a family. He chose to become personally involved in one particular little family, and what a family that was!

First there was God almighty himself, creator of the universe, then there was an unwed pregnant teenage girl, and then a very suspect older man named Joseph who was a strange one, a dreamer of dreams. Let's see, that's a dad, a step-dad, a teen-age girl, and a newborn baby all staying in a smelly barn. Not exactly your typical modern day American-culture stereo-type of what a family is supposed to be. Today, we would surely report them to county social services. The baby would be hauled off to foster parents, Joseph would probably face some very serious criminal charges, and who would believe Mary?

Who would believe Mary? I hope we do. We, with our less than perfect families, call that very troubled little family "the Holy Family," and from that family springs forth the very source of our faith and the source of our family love. Because God was there in that family, and because Mary and Joseph were willing to be used by God, that family set the standard for Christian family values. That family shepherded the shepherd for much of his life here under heaven.

Families do have problems, brothers fight, sisters offend one another so easily, spouses struggle and sometimes separate, often teenagers go through very difficult, frustrating times which cause family problems, and of course, parents do make mistakes in parenting, and even grandparents make mistakes. Still, we do our families a great disservice when we exclude them from our suffering. We withhold from them the opportunity for them to be used by God. We deny them the opportunity to rise spiritually to the occasion. Many a family rift has been healed and restored through the shared suffering of one of its members.

I would suggest that we not celebrate "Christian Family Values" so much in repudiation and defiance of family inadequacies, but in search of the love that is bigger than those inadequacies. That is the love that makes a family a family. That is the love that restores a dysfunctional family. Let our individual health crisis give us pause to savor the source of that unconditional family love.

Of course, there will be those circumstances in which a family won't or can't be there for the suffering. Then, too, some folks simply don't have families. I would suggest that the church must stand prepared to be family in the midst of one another's crisis. *"Someone told him, "Look your mother and your brothers are standing outside, wanting to speak to you." But to the one who had told him this, Jesus replied, "Who is my mother, and who are my brothers?" And pointing to his disciples, he said, "Here are my mother and my brothers! For whoever does the will of my father in heaven is my brother and sister and mother."*[21]

God has greatly blessed me with a loving family and has also given me an equally loving church family. They are family, too, and both family and church were invaluable during my surgeries and illness. At the time of my diagnosis, I had the very best work assignment to be found anywhere within the Episcopal Church. I was the Vicar of Holy Comforter Episcopal Church in Atlanta. We were a unique, one-of-a-kind inner-city mission with the parish made up of better than 70% of persons who suffer significant mental illness or organic brain damage. In addition, all subsist at or below the poverty level. Volunteers who truly live out the teachings of Christ surrounded me. Holy Comforter Mission has long presented the irony of being both a place of great suffering and a source of unfathomable faith. My little flock could not be described as simple-minded, but its members are simple-hearted. They trustingly accept God's love, power, and presence as manifest in Jesus Christ. Surely Christ had Holy Comforter in mind when he said, "*I tell you the truth, anyone who will not receive the kingdom of God like a little child, will not enter it.*"[22]

I have never known people of a more intense or more resilient faith than the folks of Holy Comforter. Not being a mental health professional, I cannot proclaim this with any authority, but as a priest, I suspect my parishioners with ill or damaged minds compensate for such by relying more intently upon their spirituality much as a blind person would rely upon his or her other senses. These folks seem to exhibit a deep spiritual sensitivity to even the more commonplace facets of everyday life. One day during our prayers, a parishioner prayed aloud, "Thank you, God, for the Atlantic Ocean." That prayer was not related to any current event or any specific dialogue, so my first reaction was to smile at its disjointed nature. I seriously doubt that thankful parishioner had even seen the Atlantic Ocean. Then, I was immediately humbled by the realization that I had never once thanked God for the Atlantic, even though that ocean had been an immeasurable source of personal delight and pleasure for much of my life.

So often, somewhat distant observers will stereotype that mission as a place of illness. Nothing could be further from the truth. Holy Comforter is first and foremost a place of awe-inspiring healing. However, one should not come to Holy Comforter seeking the entertainment of "TV Evangelism Healing." We offer a traditional Anglican form of worship. While we do offer Unction for the Sick during each worship service, most of our healing occurs in community, or more appropriately worded, "within the body." The casual observer may not even note such healing, but those who suffer do, and their faith is greatly strengthened.

Holy Comforter is a place of great courage, a place of healing, and a place of remarkable prayer. I can think of no one I'd rather have in my spiritual corner praying for my healing than my own mentally ill brothers and sisters at Holy Comforter. Again, one day during noonday prayers, I heard one of the most sacred and beautiful extemporaneous prayers I've ever heard. Someone was suffering and prayed aloud, *"Lord, I've been feelin' bad, but doin' good."* I wish I could add that powerful prayer to our prayer book. Theirs is the prayer of the "suffering," theirs is the quiet, dutiful, confident faith of the "wounded healer." Theirs is the love of Christ.

At some time following surgery, either the first or second day when I was sleeping a lot, I had a dream. It was just an ordinary dream, not some vision or mystical experience. I dreamed I was alone and frightened and wanted a hospital chaplain to come pray for me. At first, the staff seemed indifferent and unconcerned, but then their collective mood changed as they all became quite keyed up about the fact that someone had contacted the Chaplain and he was coming in person. Then I heard a real stir out in the corridor and could see nurses and doctors stepping to one side as they cleared a path for the approaching Chaplain.

I thought to myself, this Chaplain surely must be some very important person, and then I saw the Chaplain himself. Much to my surprise, it was one of our long-time parishioners who suffers extreme schizophrenia. He was wearing his usual unlaundered and food-stained clothes, his hair was a mess, and as always, his badly smudged glasses were sitting crooked upon his face. He was carrying a huge, black Bible, and I would have recognized him by his unique off-balance stride alone. It is not all that unusual to see strangers clear a path for this man, but on this day in my dream, they stepped aside for quite a different reason. They stepped aside in great awe and respect because they recognized his saintly and pure faith and hope. *"Lord, when did we see you hungry or thirsty or a stranger or needing clothes or sick or in prison?"*[23] I awoke and knew that indeed a friend had been to pray for me and visit me in my sleep.

As a clergy person, I have come to recognize that perhaps the most neglected facet of theology is the concept of friendship. Hezekiah's friends were very important to him as reflected in the poetry he penned immediately following his close brush with death. *"Never again will I see my friends or be with those who live in this world"* In John's Gospel, Jesus says, *"I do not call you servants any longer, because the servant does not know what the master is doing; but I have called you friends..."*[24] Even in the Hebrew Testament, God refers to Abraham as his friend. Although we rarely consider it as such, the model of true friendship is indeed a deeply spiritual notion. Friendship in the image of God calls us to be so much more than mere companions. God wants to be our friend, and that beckons us to be more than just pals to those closest to us. Truly good friends are a gift from God, and in that sense, I am indeed a gifted person. This illness presented me with a long over-due reminder of the spiritual value of my many friends.

Something as simple as a 'get well card' became very significant as I faced an uncertain future. I was deeply moved by one such card that harked back to my very earliest days in law enforcement. It was sent by my very first partner and training officer from back when I was a brand new rookie in 1968. A card came from my niece Paula, and that renewed a valuable long-time relationship. I think for the first time in my life, I realized just how meaningful a card could be. I even felt some sense of guilt over my past neglect to send cards as often as I should have. I'll do better in the future for, to use a popular cliché, "cards and letters poured in," and every one of them carried a very unique memory and blessing for me. From cards to prayers and personal visits, our friends went the extra mile to show us they were there for us when we needed them. Acts of kindness and compassion too numerous to inventory here will remain with me throughout my life.

Dan and Kathy are long-lasting friends whom we see often throughout the year even though miles separate us. They were among the very first persons I called out to for help when I was first diagnosed and most uncertain about all that was happening to me. Not only are they very close personal friends, they offered special insight and firsthand knowledge and experience into just what I was going through. Kathy works with the provision of healthcare services and Dan is a colon cancer survivor who came very close to death a few years ago while undergoing treatment at the Mayo Clinic in Rochester, Minnesota. Throughout that struggle, Dan maintained a most positive and confident attitude and thus expected a like response from me. Having gone through much of what I experienced, Dan was also invaluable in keeping me posted as to just what to expect next. Dan and Kathy came to Atlanta to be with Judy and me following my release from the hospital and during that exasperating and uncertain waiting for the pathology results. They coached humor, patience, and hopefulness, and turned our thoughts to the more positive aspects of the ordeal.

Then there is yet another very special friend who was there for me with an absolutely amazing insight into what Judy and I experienced. Sue was actually a friend and a co-worker who managed and/or coordinated the finances and business affairs at Holy Comforter parish. On occasions, I had to call her at home on one of her days off, and if she was not in, I would get an answering machine and hear the voice of her husband, the Rev. B. Fred Hannan, inviting me to leave a message. I then usually just hung up and called her on her cell phone if it was important. Later on, though, I was very tempted to leave a message for Fred. That message would say, "Thank you, Fred, for your courage and faith and love. Your very recent ministry to me has been vital to my faith, hope, and peace of mind. You have an absolutely wonderful family who are a real credit to your life and your continued positive influence." I was tempted to leave that message; but I didn't. Instead, I took care of it with a prayer. You see, Fred died about three years prior to my diagnosis; the cause of his death was Renal Cell Carcinoma.

"Moses ordained him, and anointed him with holy oil; it was an everlasting covenant for him and for his descendants as long as the heavens endure, to minister to the Lord and serve as priest and bless his people in his name."[25] I carry a small vial of scented olive oil which was blessed by a bishop and is used for anointing those seeking prayer for divine healing. It belonged to Fred, and he diligently used it for that purpose in his ministry as a priest. I've noticed of late that the supply of oil is dwindling; it will not last forever. But God's covenant will last as long as the heavens endure and so will Fred's ministry. In that ministry, he followed Christ's advice to store up for himself treasures in heaven. His hard work, care, and compassion certainly didn't net him great material treasure here on earth; his treasure was where his heart was, and that was with his family and serving and blessing God and God's people.

I understand why Sue would not change that recorded message. Sue understood my deepest fears during the absolute darkest days of my illness. Needless to say, when she counseled me about all I had been going through, I listened. She knows. Sue was my valued co-worker, my friend, and a wise counselor. Fred is my hero.

Anguish and Mental Suffering

"I waited patiently all night, but I was torn apart as though by lions. Delirious, I chattered like a swallow or a crane, and I moaned like a morning dove. My eyes grew tired of looking to heaven for help."

I had family, friends, church, and eventually a really good doctor; God provided just what I needed as I needed it. None-the-less, like Hezekiah, I was emotionally anxious and stressed and called out to God for help. *"Am I to be robbed of the rest of my years? I said, never again will I see the Lord God while still in the land of the living."* I had and still have strong faith, and I'm a good enough actor to have feigned self-serving courage. However, Christianity suffers enough hypocrisy as it is. And it is never well served by anything less than total honesty from its adherents. Then, too, the ultimate harm in feigned courage might be realized in the subsequent temptation to con even myself. Facing death is painful. I can't imagine anything worse than confronting it with a contrived and bogus courage for the imagined sake of others. First and foremost, others deserve the truth about us. I know facing cancer takes both faith and courage, but neither faith nor courage can be artificially contrived without dire consequences. If my fears and distress appear less than valiant, then so be it. As Merton writes, *"Heroism alone is useless, unless it is born by God."*[26]

I remember when I first encountered the word "cancer" when, as a young boy, I went with my dad to visit a man from our church who had cancer. On the way, I asked my dad, "What is cancer?" He told me it was a deadly disease with no known cure. He explained to me the doctors had performed surgery on this man, had found him full of cancer, and had sent him home to die. The man we were visiting was dying. My dad was a loving, sensitive man who must have detected my fear that afternoon. As he pulled our relatively new 1952 Studebaker to the curb in front of the "cancer man's" house, he said, "I won't be long, do you just want to wait in the car?" Needless to say, I was relieved, but perhaps waiting alone in the car as Daddy went into that "cancer house" was not my best option.

It seems like I have spent a lifetime in that car, trying to avoid familiarity with, if not knowledge and understanding of, the disease. I've spent a lifetime afraid of cancer. I was spiritually intimidated by the ghost of a physical disease. That fearsome ghost was nothing more than a simple lack of information. In very recent years, local radio and television stations have started carrying spot advertising for cancer treatment centers. At first, I found those ads depressing and strangely out of place there among the shrill voices of all the auto dealership con men. Now those ads bring me comfort. Now that I have experienced the disease, I regret all those years of fear when I kept the topic at such a distance. I am most thankful for my recent years as an Episcopal Priest when I've worked so closely with those who were either dying from or surviving cancer. They are my heroes–they are my saints; they were there for me during the worst of my fears, and they will be my companions for the rest of this life journey. The ones I've done last rites for will be there cheering me on as I inevitably stumble across that glorious finish line and fall into the open arms of God.

Paige was one such saint/hero who has been there and

is still there for me. I was so impressed with her faith and courage that I asked for permission to publicly use her story, and she consented without hesitation. I've already used her life's witness in sermons and am confident I will do so again in the future. Little did I realize though, that I would be using her story and experience to strengthen and sustain my own faith in the face of my own cancer diagnosis. Paige was an active young parishioner who would undergo chemo-therapy early on Sunday mornings and then make it to church for the 10:30 AM service. When physically able, she would come to Holy Comforter during the week to assist with the mentally ill and our parish-gardening program. One day, she asked for a specific appointment to talk to me about "something important." She arrived on time and once seated in my office, explained that her cancer had worsened and the doctors had given her just four more months to live. She did die in just about four months, and I administered extreme unction for her in a hospital room just down from the one I occupied following my first surgery.

She didn't mince words the day of her appointment. She simply told me she didn't have time to waste. She wanted me to explain how she could know she was going to heaven. We talked about trust and faith as our appropriate free will response to love given by an unseen God whose very essence is love. We talked about repentance, and then we went to the Book of Common Prayer and both renewed our baptismal vows complete with those wonderful interrogatories. Do you renounce Satan? Do you renounce the evil powers of this world? Do you renounce sinful desires? Do you turn to Jesus Christ and accept him as your Savior? Do you put your whole trust in His grace and love? Do you promise to follow and obey Him as your Lord? Paige very honestly answered all of those questions in the affirmative, and in her own answers, she found her blessed assurance. Then we turned to the back of the book and reviewed some of the specific prayers, and there she found the Prayer attributed to St. Francis and that very compelling line, *"and it is in dying that we are born to eternal life."* She loved that prayer, and she was at peace.

Like Paige, we will find our strength and our peace in our faith. Those who prioritize knowledge over love often claim our faith is a result of our fear. They will say, "You're afraid of dying, so you conjure up your faith in response to that fear." They say such because it is in that limited realm of human intellect that they live and move and have their being. I've been with too many dying people to agree with that diminutive and oft times silly one-dimensional human thinking. I don't believe our faith comes from our fear. I think it comes from our need for strength which in turn comes from a source that is larger than our thought process and/or our knowledge. Contrary to some human thinking, humankind is not the top of the intellectual food chain. *"Fools say in their hearts, there is no God."*[27] Simply put, our faith, and thus our strength, comes from a God that is love. Ours is a spiritual strength that survives knowledge and biological death. Ours is a spiritual strength that resists our subjection to irrational fear even in the face of cancer. Our faith is our armor.

For many of the years we lived in Atlanta, Judy and I celebrated New Years at our friends, Dan and Kathy's, bed & breakfast on Spirit Lake in Iowa. Not many people vacation in northern Iowa in January. Spirit Lake had always been completely frozen over during our winter visits. But such was not the case one particular year. That year, a large portion of the lake remained open. You see, several thousand– and I am not exaggerating – several thousand Canadian Geese decided to winter over at Spirit Lake that year. They found abundant grain in the stubble of the near-by harvested fields and were constantly flying out to those fields and back to the lake. Their collective body temperature and their constant movement churning the waters kept that portion of the lake from freezing over. I was fascinated by those geese and sat by the fire and watched them for hours.

Holy Scripture tells of Jesus' baptism and how the Holy Spirit descended from the sky like a dove. It wasn't a dove, it was the Holy Spirit, but it descended bodily like a dove. Thus, the dove is a symbol of the Holy Spirit. Very early Christian Missionaries traveled to the northern most regions of Ireland and told the locals this story of the descending dove. The local's reaction to the story was, "What's a dove?" It seems there was no doves that far north. The missionaries then improvised, and so to this day, we find an occasional descending wild goose amid our Christian Symbols. The Celts could understand the meaning and power of Christ's Baptism when they were told that the Holy Spirit descended from the sky like a wild goose. The symbol of the dove held no special meaning for them, but they had seen geese descending from the sky, and now I have, too; and now I know the beauty and the strength of that Celtic symbol.

That winter, the v-shaped flights of geese would usually come in low across the frozen portion of the lake, gliding for long distances only a foot or two above the ice. But occasionally, a flight would come in very high, and it was almost as if the lead goose would look down and say, "Oops! That's where we want to go, right below us." He or she would raise the front edge of one wing slightly, which would catch the wind, and that wind would flip that goose over into a sort of side-ways summersault. The others followed as they then flew straight down like a group of World War II dive-bombers. As they neared the surface, their wings would arc more like an open parachute than an airplane wing as they would gently settle into the frigid waters of Spirit Lake.

The sheer strength and resilience of those big birds renewed my faith in the strength and the resilience of our Christian faith. The wild goose is one tough bird; not a mean bird nor a predator, but a strong one none-the-less. The rougher the elements, the harsher the environment, the more the goose seems to thrive. That same spirit of strength and faith has been lived out in the lives of my cancer heroes. I think the same is true of our personal faith in confronting cancer.

The day I learned of my diagnosis of cancer, I returned home, grabbed my prayer book, and found a little solitude. I very specifically replicated that meeting with Paige. I repeated the prayers and reflections and asked God to give me some of Paige's courage and peace. That day, Paige ministered to me from glory. Pondering my work with Paige, I now reflect upon my fitness to minister to her as she faced her death. How could I effectively help her deal with something I had yet to work through in my own personal life? Who was ministering to whom? I am confident my prayers and my words helped her prepare for life after death. I know her faith was strengthened. But did I or could I bring any comfort to her in preparation for death itself?

Harold Koenig and Andrew Weaver write in their handbook for pastors and religious caregivers, *"It is critical that you work through your personal issues with death before you offer yourself in ministry to the dying. Becoming truly involved requires the risk of identifying with the person in pain and may awaken deep-seated fears and unresolved conflicts that can lead to emotional turmoil in the helper. It is impossible to be present for others in times of grief and suffering when you are caught up in your own hidden emotions."*[28] While theirs is indeed a relevant and helpful writing, I do find myself in disagreement with the forgoing specific approach to caring for the dying.

They present "identifying with the dying" as a "risk" as though the pastor was a therapist rather than a shepherd. I believe this methodical and sterile sounding advice presupposes managing mortality to be a clinical and intellectual exercise or process. It is not; it is a deeply spiritual phenomenon to be experienced on God's time schedule. The shepherd must identify with the sheep.

We're not talking therapy here, for such would require each dying person to have a personal therapist. I believe it is possible for those dealing with their own emotions to be present for others in times of suffering. It was not 'impossible' for the "Wounded Healer" of the Talmud to be present for others in times of grief and suffering. He was not without wounds; in fact, his own wounds were the source of healing. He didn't keep them hidden; he kept them bound so he could respond quickly to those in need of ministry. Henri Nowen writes, "*A Christian community is therefore a healing community not because wounds are cured and pains are alleviated, but because wounds and pains become openings or occasions for new vision. Mutual confession then becomes a mutual deepening of hope, and sharing weakness becomes a reminder to one and all of the coming strength.*"[29] Mutual confession is the work of a pastor rather than that of a therapist.

Koenig and Weaver write, "*It is impossible to be present for others in times of grief and suffering when you are caught up in your own hidden emotions.*" I must ask, "Why should we try to hide our own emotions concerning our own death? Isn't that precisely the problem?" What seems to me to be impossible is the advice for pastors to work through their personal issues with death before offering themselves in ministry to the dying. Let's be practical here. If nothing else, death requires honest, open practicality. Our young pastors are expected to "hit the ground running." In fact, those from the main-line denominations are required to successfully complete 'Clinical Pastoral Education' prior to graduation from seminary. This program places the young seminarian in a pastoral role within hospitals and hospices. It is a course of preparation, but the folks they minister to are not training manikins or role players. They are real people, and the seminarians become real pastors to them as they face death or the threat of death. CPE is not a "dry run."

It seems to me the hiding of personal emotions would

present a far greater problem than any sort of failure to completely work through one's personal fears of the biological process of death. Jesus openly wept at the grave of his friend Lazarus and then later sweats blood while working through his own pending death. Apparently, Christ had worked through his relationship with the Father but had not worked through his personal issues with death to the point that he was prepared to always present a polished, unshaken image in the face of suffering and grief. He was truly human and so are pastors and other religious caregivers. They can bring comfort to the dying by sharing in the suffering and simultaneously sharing their hope in the face of their own fears and weaknesses. Of course, the pastor should not dwell upon his or her own suffering to the extent that it detracts from the needs of others. I would suggest there is an easily achieved balance here to be found in the sensitivity of a loving care-giver.

When Hezekiah built his tunnel to carry healing waters from the Kidron Valley to the Pool of Siloam, he sent two teams down to start tunneling toward each other from opposite directions. With apparently little more than rough measurements and certainly without modern scientific devices to keep them on track, they tunneled their way through the dark earth toward each other. As the teams neared each other, they would pause in their digging to shout and then listen for the sounds of the other team. It was indeed a miracle that they actually met to connect and thus complete the waterway. What a joyous celebration that meeting must have been.

I see pastoral care for the dying in much the same light as the construction of Hezekiah's Tunnel. The pastor is certainly not Hezekiah commissioning and monitoring from a distant palace. Neither is he or she a modern day engineer sent down to give scientific guidance. The pastor does not possess the tools for that expert role. Again, the pastoral care giver is most likely not trained and or equipped to provide therapy. The pastor is a child of the earth and must get down into the dust of the tunnel and work toward dying and death with the dying. While not the recipient of the care, he or she is working toward the same location in much the same mode. The pastoral counselor must dig a little, pause to listen a lot, and on occasion, shout out his or her faith and hope to be heard by the other.

The pastoral counselor is not a therapist. As I understand it, professional therapeutic care is one-directional in its commitment to the suffering and is most helpful in many of life's circumstances. With therapy, I understand that the therapist's feelings and experiences don't count. However, that very characteristic that makes therapy so effective in so many circumstances is not well suited for work with the dying. One directional digging is required for digging graves. Focusing attention solely upon the fears, despair, and suffering of the dying can seem lonely, cold, and sterile. It tends to deny the fact that we are all dying. Two directional digging by two teams (community) is best for digging tunnels rather than graves. Mutually shared faith is sure to be the light at the end of the tunnel. The realization that *"we are all in this thing together"* brings a sense of and the real presence of community. We are all building the same tunnel. It is my opinion and experience that the dying most prefer honesty, openness, and sincerity over professionalism. They prefer love over sophisticated counseling skills. I think they prefer the wounded healer over the neutral therapist. Doubtlessly, some need both.

One of my seminary professors confided that, as a young pastor, a child died in his small, rural, and remote Nevada congregation. He conducted the funeral service but began to cry as he began his sermon. He tried but just couldn't proceed, and a layman took over and did an admirable job of preaching an extemporaneous sermon. Following the service, my professor apologized profusely to the parents who insisted he not apologize. The child's father said, "We now know you share our pain and love our child." The tunnel met there in the darkness. Our wise instructor told us those tears were one of his very best sermons ever. That course was entitled "Introduction to Pastoral Care." I now know enough about pastoral care to realize the effective pastor does not pontificate holy philosophy in the face of death, rather we are called to share life, joy, faith, death, suffering, and grief. We are primarily called to share the love of Christ.

My previous experiences with Paige and other cancer victims were a source of great pastoral comfort. Then, too, I was blessed with priests and even bishops who loved and ministered to me as I wrestled with the fear of dying. Oddly enough, the one key person missing from my support team was a doctor with the time available to listen to my fears. I know that is a lot to expect. I'm sure that first urologist is an excellent surgeon and physician, but I will never know his personal friendship and care first hand. I sought a second opinion, and thus God sent me a truly great doctor in a rather unusual fashion.

One day after my surgery, the urology resident was leading the interns or med students on their rounds and introduced me as the man who had his kidney removed by his pharmacist. We all laughed, as they knew their Urology Professor had long ago started as a pharmacist in a small family-owned drug store in suburban Mableton, Georgia. They knew that my surgeon had both an MD and a PharmD following his name. They also knew he continued to fill in four hours per week as a substitute pharmacist at that same store as a unique means of keeping up with the ever-changing medications prescribed and used in urology. I guess other docs rely upon journal articles and pharmaceutical sales staff to keep them updated. Jeff does likewise, but from behind the pharmacy counter, he can also see firsthand the trends in meds and treatments and can speak with a wide range of patients and receive their honest and forthright feedback about the specifics of the different treatments.

I had always preferred small independent pharmacies in which I could get to know the pharmacist and thus have another source of information about my health. This became doubly important to me upon being diagnosed with Type-II diabetes in 1998. On my daily way to and from seminary, I would pass the small stand-alone Mableton Pharmacy, so I started to take my prescriptions there and found the family that owned and operated it to be very friendly, sincere, and loving Baptists. There is nothing quite as stimulating as a conversation between a committed Episcopalian and a committed Baptist who both realize God is very real and does expect us to respect and love one another. It also helps to incorporate a little sense of humor into theological discussions. Thus, we became good friends, and they took both a personal and a professional interest in my health issues and in me.

However, the family did not work Saturdays when I was most often free to go in and pick up my meds. A young man who served as a substitute pharmacist covered Saturday mornings. I liked Jeff, a native-born Georgian, and I would lean against the counter and talk with him when the store was not busy. He seemed very bright, and I never knew why, but he had lived and studied in both Virginia and San Francisco. Thus we shared some common interests and geography.

I went in to the pharmacy during the week to pick up some new meds and asked them to be praying for me as I told them of my newly discovered tumor. I explained to them that the doctor who found the tumor was triple-booked and could squeeze me in for follow-up consultation and additional tests in seven days at the soonest. By that time, I knew how fast acting, aggressive, and dangerous some cancer of the kidney could be, and I was scared and frustrated. The pharmacists sensed this and told me, "You need to talk to Jeff."

I asked, "Why; does he know a good doctor who could see me sooner?"

Much to my surprise, they answered, "Jeff is a good doctor! This is not commonly known around here, but Jeff is Dr. K. Jeffrey Carney, the Chief of Urology at Grady Memorial Hospital." Grady is the large Trauma Center Hospital in downtown Atlanta. They continued to explain that Jeff was also a Professor of Urology at Emory University Medical School. Coincidentally, Emory University is where I graduated from seminary, but Emory, of course, is better known for its medical school and research hospital, The Winship Cancer Institute and its new Center of Cancer Nanotechnology, and primarily, as the site of the international Centers for Disease Control.

I knew my friends and pharmacists to be honest people not prone to exaggeration, but still, I was so surprised I went straight home, got on the Internet, and confirmed all that they had told me. Saturday morning I was back at the pharmacy, and Jeff and I had a long talk. He is a man who exudes hope and confidence, and he reassured me that morning that he would take care of me. He gave me his personal cell number and long encouraged me to call him at any hour. He was single and so has relatively few family responsibilities, which is good because he is in surgery at least three days a week. I am concerned that he is able to find sufficient time for himself, but his work is healing, and he is one who does not prioritize personal wealth over faith and service to others. Just knowing Jeff and the folks at the Mableton Pharmacy is a blessing and an answer to prayer. Those who commit their lives to such noble crusades are unsung heroes who warrant our continued prayers. I find this all more than a refreshing little story of a good physician and a caring local pharmacy. It is a strong testimony of intense dedication to the art of healing and the quality of our medical profession at a time when such seems so rare.

So in a few short days, I did find a highly qualified urologist who took the time to talk to me and reassure me. He even met with me on that Saturday morning outside of his normal office hours. However, he did not have immediate access to my test results and had to be frank and honest with me; it could be very bad for me. At one point in the conversation, he reached over and simply placed his hand on my arm and said, "Mark, don't worry. I am going to take very good care of you." It may sound naïve or superficial, but that simple gesture offered me great solace. What is there in the elemental human touch that seems so mystical in the healing process? That was a pivotal point in my adjustment to all that was happening to me. I had found the scrap of hope I was looking for. Prior to that, those first few early days were a time of tough, gut-wrenching adjustment.

A Call for Help

⌇

Hezekiah pleads, "*I am in trouble, Lord. Help me.*" Question: How does a sufferer call out to God for help? Answer: Very softly, for God is right there in the suffering. He doesn't cause it, but He is right there in the midst of suffering. My cancer heroes (survivors or not), my pastors, my wounded "Holy Comforter" flock, my loving family, my long-time friends, my dog Talbot, my doctors, nurses, and techs, and a man named Jesus are all my traveling companions now. If so casually tossing in the name "Jesus" makes me sound "fundamentalist," then so be it. But please know that I won't be easily labeled. It may sound apathetic, but nothing could be less important to me now than religious labels. Nothing could be more important than Christ's love for me and my returned love for Christ. I was shocked, frightened, frustrated, and suffering. I initially tried to handle all of that on my own and found I couldn't. I asked for God's help, and God was there to rescue me. He primarily worked through others and his creation to do so. In fact, at times, I couldn't separate the love of friends, family, and care givers from God's love and salvation. I think that's the way it should be. None-the-less, Christ was present in the Holy Comforter. He is my friend, he is my strength, and he is my hope and my redeemer. I worship him in spirit and in truth.

I do disdain labels; but I am a Christian and a priest, so my use of the name "Jesus" should come as no great surprise to anyone. I make no apologies. But then neither should it offend anyone. I am aware that Christ never forced himself on anyone. He is the very essence of love, and there is no such thing as forced love. So I want to be very careful not to throw that name in anyone's face. He is my friend, not my weapon. I strive to be a loving priest, not a fighting soldier in some culture-driven political arena. Christ is my travelling companion up close and personal.

During my six-year tenure as a jail chaplain, I learned to respect other faiths, especially those faiths directed to the God of Abraham. I even learned to respect the dignity and wishes of those who personally choose to completely reject any form of faith for their lives. It is their decision to make, and not even God would take that choice from them. My response to those who reject any form of faith is to sincerely respect them, do my best to live out the gospel, and pray that they will ultimately make the choices that conform to God's will for them.

I have long subscribed to the old folk-adage that there are no atheists in foxholes, and thus trust that God, time, and the events of this life will eventually catch up with those who lack faith. Now that I know what it is like to find oneself in a foxhole in the brutal battle against cancer, I believe that adage more than ever. If persons of no faith broach the subject of faith with me, then of course I will be the priest and proclaim the Gospel. But, generally I tend to leave the timing and the heavy work to the Holy Spirit. We claim to be a people who believe in prayer; we should do more prayer and less in-your-face evangelism. Prayer ought to be the major portion of our evangelism.

My personal prayers for help seemed to bring God very close to me during that time of anguish. I not only related to God through the church, but also personally and directly. Ultimately, the close and personal presence of Christ most effectively vanquished any mental anguish I may have suffered concerning my dilemma. There is a favorite song of mine written by Julie Gold and made popular a few years back by one of my favorite entertainers, Bette Midler. The key phrase is, "God is watching us" & the title is "From a Distance." I love the tune, and you will hear me humming it from time to time, even though I don't carry a tune very well. However, in my generation's best tradition, I can only give my favorite song a "Seven." I like the tune, but it's difficult to dance to that theology of a distant God.

Those of us who have suffered and know and love a God, who is love, find it difficult to dance to the deist theology of a far-removed God. There are those who would have us believe God is distant simply because they are more comfortable with a distant God. Really, who wants God leaning over our shoulder watching every move we make when things are going so well, and we are busy doing our own thing? At times, it does seem nice to imagine a God watching us from a safe and not-too-involved distance. Perhaps He could just check in once-in-a-while to see that all is going well with us as he sort of channel surfs His whole creation.

A distant God may seem very attractive during easy times, but in a life threatening personal health crisis, we appreciate a close God who is personally involved in our pain. We take comfort in Holy Scripture which reveals a God who has always wanted to be close to His people. He walked through the Garden of Eden in search of Adam and Eve. He found them and that unfortunate incident with the fruit of the forbidden tree, and so God became distant. But as with any loving parent, God loved and missed the kids and couldn't tolerate the distance. So He had his children build a tent, and then a temple was built just so he could dwell among them. God moved back into the neighborhood.

But wouldn't you know that still wasn't close enough for God. He wanted to be even closer yet, so He became a man and stepped onto the stage of human history. But that was really too close for human comfort, so we crucified and buried him. But he rose again and ascended to be with the Father. Even then, He was not about to leave his kids home alone. His ascension cleared the path for the Holy comforter and Pentecost. Pentecost was that point in human history when our God really became an up close and personal kind of God. That day God moved in with us. Suffering or not, the personal immanence or nearness of God is indeed a beautiful theme. It is the principle theme of Christmas, Easter, and Pentecost. It is the principle theme of the Eucharist and Baptism and all of the lesser sacraments.

Christ was God made human. Christ is God made close. Jesus didn't distance himself from anyone, not the tax collectors, not the thieves, not the prostitutes, not the destitute, not the sick, not even the insane. He was close enough for that woman to reach out and touch the hem of His garment; he was close enough for small, noisy, dirty-faced children to climb onto His lap; he was close enough for Peter to reach out and grab as Peter was sinking beneath the waves of his own doubt. He is still close enough for us to reach out and grab a hold of in our battle with cancer.

The untouchables of his day were the lepers who were absolutely forbidden by law from reaching out to touch anyone, but Jesus was just close enough to reach out and touch their rotting flesh. He not only touched them; he touched them with love and with healing. He was close enough for a sinful woman to drench his feet in her tears; and alas, he was close enough for Judas to kiss. In our illness and suffering, we know not some far and distant God who sees only our planet and humanity in general. We still worship that up close and personal God of the lepers. We worship a God who dwells among us here in this place; one who lives with us and in us and through us.

In our suffering, we do sense God nearby, but I think it is difficult for us to truly comprehend just how close God is to us. Paul writes in First Corinthians, "For now we see in a mirror dimly, but then face to face." That line reminds me of my theologically correct Jeep. I rather doubt St. Paul etched it there, but one day, I looked over and saw a little godly message in the passenger-side rear-view mirror. I don't know how it got there; it's almost as though it came from the factory that way. There printed right in the glass it reads: "Objects in mirror are closer than they appear." I can pull out on the highway and look in that mirror and see a Mack truck approaching in the distance. Then I'm always surprised to look over my shoulder and see nothing but a large chrome grill up close; and so it is with God. He can seem so distant at times, but today, we can still reach out and touch the hem of his garment. He is there for us because He loves us. He is there for us because He is love. He is love, and he is life.

Hezekiah composed, *"Yes, this anguish was good for me, for you have rescued me from death; and forgiven all my sins."*[30] Thus, this Old Testament king closely tied death to sin and life to forgiveness. While our disease and suffering are not sin, those of us who suffer life threatening disease are not without sin and stand in need of forgiveness. Of course, the same can be said of those who are not suffering. However, with life so closely associated with forgiveness, perhaps forgiveness takes on a new urgency for those dealing with the threat of natural death.

I have been a Christian believer all my life, even during times when my behavior didn't reflect that persistent core faith. Without wallowing in my offenses, let me assure you they were significant to a pure and holy God. They were significant to others. Still, my childhood belief in Christ was ever present. Perhaps it is due to God's abundant forgiveness for me, but I don't believe the core principles of Christianity are *"good and bad,"* rather, I believe they are *"life and death."* While right living obviously plays a central role, the Christian faith is not all about Jesus coming to town to find out who's been naughty and who's been nice. That's Santa Claus, not Christ. We confuse the two at our own spiritual peril. To reduce God to nothing more than a simple choice between right and wrong is to make God's love conditional, and that openly invites others to negatively impact, hamper, and frustrate our relationship with God. God and God's forgiveness are close and easily accessible without legalistic and judgmental self-appointed mediators dictating the conditions of our relationship with God based upon their experiences. God does not clone believers.

Certainly God wants us to behave ourselves. He wants us to choose to do so out of love, not out of fear or in compliance to enforceable rules and regulations. God makes spiritual freedom, not doctrinal cages! Christianity is not primarily about living a good life, rather it's about living. It's not all about good and bad; it's about life and death. It's about choosing eternal life over death. Again I cite Thomas Merton, *"Our whole life should be a meditation of our last and most important decision: the choice between life and death. We must all die. But the dispositions with which we face death make our death a choice either of death or of life. If, during our life we have chosen life, then in death we will pass from death to life."*[31]

"Those who believe in me, even though they die, will live." Jesus was talking to Lazarus' sister Martha, when he said this, and then he followed up by asking her a very personal question. *"Martha, do you believe this?"* Note that He didn't ask her, "Have you been behaving yourself, Martha?" I don't want to diminish the significance of righteous living, but He knew she was not without sin – she was not perfect. But that clearly was not his primary concern at that time. Martha was grieving the death of her brother, so he asked, *"Do you believe?"* That's an Easter question. That's a question of life and death. Questions of good and bad always lead to principled legalism which, in turn, frequently leads

to death. It did in Christ's ministry. Questions of Life and death, on the other hand, lead to faith and love. Our faith cannot be separated from His forgiving grace.

One would expect that a sixty-year-old clergy person would be in touch with his own mortality. I think I was in touch with the eventual reality of it all. I accepted death as much as anyone could while maintaining a reasonable and wholesome hope for a normal life span. I understood that my eventual biological demise was inevitable and part of this life. It was something to be expected eventually. My faith offered a great expectation of eternal spiritual life, so I really never feared the afterlife. I had even found myself in somewhat frequent life-threatening circumstances during the early years of my law enforcement career. I was always cautious and very aware of the danger and the potential for sudden death. But sudden death would be sudden, and I could handle sudden. I seemed in control, and somehow that, too, made a difference. I must confess to actually finding a little youthful but very foolish thrill in the excitement, danger, and the risk of it all.

This formal diagnosis of Renal Cell Carcinoma presented absolutely no such thrill or sense of adventure at all. It robbed me of any control and initially slammed me hard against my own faith. I had to first recognize that I was completely helpless and hopeless. I had to give up and accept a foreseeable termination of this life, even though it was only a possibility for me at that time. For me, it ceased to be a matter of life or death and became a question of my forced surrender to death sooner rather than later. Regardless of what the tests would eventually show, regardless of just what my life expectancy really was, the question became "was I prepared for the death process?" I struggled mentally and emotionally with that fundamental question and realized that, like Hezekiah, not only was I not prepared to die; there was absolutely nothing I could do to prepare for my own death. There was a lot God could do to prepare me to die, but nothing I could do, no mental strategy or thought process I could conjure up to facilitate preparation for death.

Some would argue that "Yes, there is something we can do to prepare for death; we must repent and be saved." To those folks, I respond that you are referring to preparation for life after death, not death. You are brushing over biological death as though it were not a reality and a significant part of this life. You may be in personal denial. Your evangelism is admirable, but your love seems a little disingenuous. Now let me clarify here that I do understand Christ's teaching about the necessity of spiritual re-birth. While I disagree with a dogmatic, lockstep by-the-numbers, neat little pre-packaged one-size-fits-all process required for the achievement of such re-birth, I do embrace the teachings of Christ in this matter whole-heartedly. I strongly recommend it for others.

The evangelical stock-in-trade question, *"If you died today, where would you go?"* trivializes my "dying today." Christ didn't trivialize his own death; why would anyone so casually dismiss mine? It seems an odd question you so nonchalantly ask, and just why would you ask something that so smacks of your judgment and condemnation? Fear of hell does not make for an appropriate introduction to the Prince of Peace.

I think we are all capable of fearing death, and I suspect we believers have played on this fear far more than we have championed God's love and mercy. Nothing so clearly reveals this proclivity for heavy-handed fear-mongering quite like the Book of Common Prayer used by the Episcopal Church from 1892 to 1928. That prayer book characteristically presents a bone-chilling proclamation intended for use by jail and prison chaplains when escorting a condemned person to the gallows. It reads in part:

"Dearly beloved, it hath pleased almighty God, in his justice, to bring you under the sentence and condemnation of the law. You are shortly to suffer death in such a manner, that others may be the more afraid to offend; and we pray God, that you may make such use of your punishments in this world, that your soul may be saved in the world to come.

Wherefore we come to you in the bowels of compassion; and being, desirous that you should avoid presumption on the one hand, and despair on the other, shall plainly lay before you the wretchedness of your condition, and declare how far you ought to depend on the mercies of God and the merits of our Savior. Consider then seriously with yourself, in all appearance the time of your dissolution draweth near; your sins have laid fast hold on you; you are soon to be removed from among men by a violent death; and you shall fade away like grass, which in the morning is green and groweth up, but in the evening is cut down, dried up and withered. After you have thus finished the course of a sinful and miserable life, you shall appear before the judge of all flesh; who, as he pronounces blessings on the righteous, shall likewise say, with a terrible voice of most just judgment, to the wicked, Go ye accursed, into the fire everlasting, prepared for the devil and his angels."[32]

Such is the history of the church in counseling condemned persons facing a looming execution and an eminent death. And yet Jesus merely said to the condemned man,

"Truly I tell you, today you will be with me in paradise."[33] Quite some difference, huh? The institutional church and criminally condemned prisoners aside, fear of death makes for a lousy evangelical tool for any one, and that task is best left to the Holy Spirit whose job is to convict persons of the need to repent. The Spirit has a very high job performance rating in that area of its work responsibility and will do a far better job than we. While there are times when the Spirit will make it quite clear to us that our assistance is appropriately called for, I suspect that most of the time we need only provide a good witness with our life, a little love, and a lot of prayer. The great commission is alive and well and cannot be reduced to a canned sales pitch.

Repent and be saved indeed! I did repent, I do repent, and I will repent. And I was saved more than 2000 years ago at a place called Golgotha, and I personally accept the love, grace, and sacrifice inherent in that deadly and painful crucifixion. But still, I was not prepared for this phase of my own existence to end. I dearly loved this life and wanted to cling to it. I still do to this day. Thus, I was not prepared for my own biological death. I was not spiritually or mentally primed for my personal dying process.

In John's Gospel, we read, *"Those who love their life will loose it, and those who hate their life in this world will keep it for eternal life."*[34] King Hezekiah loved life and feared death. I'm afraid that I must confess that I, too, love this life. I love my wife, I love my kids, I love my friends, I love my church, I love my work. I consider them all gifts from God, and I love God's gifts given in love. God has richly blessed me, and I love it. I don't hate this life, but Jesus says there in John that those who hate their life in this world will keep it for eternal life. Sort of reminds us of His teaching, "Whoever comes to me and does not hate father and mother, wife and children, brother and sister, yes even life itself, cannot be my disciple." He taught that even though he simultaneously demonstrated great love and respect for His own mother Mary. What parent would purposely teach their young children to hate this life? Yet, at first blush, that seems to be Christ's message in John's 12ᵗʰ Chapter.

This is indeed a difficult teaching for those who would take a literal approach to all Holy Scripture; that is, if we proof-text this particular passage to the exclusion of Christ's other teachings. You interpret and apply this passage as you choose; that's your valuable and precious free prerogative as a child of God. However, I don't believe Christ contradicts himself here at all. This is not a stand-alone verse. I believe His words here must be taken against a back-drop of his very own great commandments: Love God first and foremost, and then Love others, and love self. This begs the question, "How can we hate our life if our life is love?" How can we hate our existence if we follow and obey his great commandments to love? If our existence is a proper prioritization and a spiritually healthy balance of love for God, love for others, and love for ourselves, how can we hate it?

In the context of that chapter, these radical and demanding words of caution reflect an urgent priority of the Kingdom. "The hour has come!" Many who heard these same words when they were first proclaimed were called to a ministry of martyrdom. God called them to die for the faith. They faced torture and horrible deaths for the sake of the newly established Kingdom in the months and years that immediately followed these statements of life and death. What seems to be difficult wording for us from our blessed and comfortable 21st century vantage point may have sounded very encouraging to those first century disciples. Would I have so dearly loved a life of severe persecution and death by stoning? Of course, there are still places in this world where Christians are yet called to die for their faith. Then, too, there may be times in our lives when we actually do hate this phase of life.

The temptations and spiritual traps of a comfortable,

convenient, and blessed life can lead to a "me, me, and more of me" attitude. As such, it becomes very tempting to love this life more than I love an unseen God of faith. At times, it is tempting to make this life my God; that is to separate love from faith. Now, a life that takes precedence over that kind of love for others is indeed detestable. I should hate life when it becomes so self-centered that it is all about me and more of me. I can love myself but never love myself more than I love God. We call that sin.

Then, too, I think some of this radical sounding bend simply comes from Christ's role as a master teacher. We should remember that he was a teacher without text-books, highlight markers, or hand-outs. There were no Xerox machines. No power-point presentations. No sound systems. Jesus didn't have a web site up and running. He was the living word and was teaching a curriculum of life and death. He desperately wanted his teaching points to stick and to be forever retained by his students. After all, these were crucially important concepts. The listener had to know, understand, and remember this. I guess he could have said something like, "Prioritize obedience over the fleeting pleasures of life." But then that mediocre wording would probably be quickly overwhelmed by the teachings of others. Those words just don't have the impact or staying power or fortitude of, "those who hate their life in this world will keep it." Now that's something to remember.

Those words reach out and grab me because I love this life. The truth of the matter is God is love, and if we put our love for that God of love in the proper perspective and priority, we will encounter no conflict between love of that God and love of life. Again, it was this same great teacher that taught us to live our lives loving God, neighbor, and self.

Hate this life! In proclaiming such, Christ was leading to a follow-up proclamation, "*Whoever serves me must follow me, and where I am, there will my servant be also.*"[35] This, too, is a difficult teaching lesson. Oh, it wasn't all that difficult to follow Christ around Galilee, to the top of the mountain, out in the boat, or into Jerusalem itself. But now Christ is traveling toward his crucifixion, to his death, and he is still saying, "Follow Me!" and we don't want to because sometimes our love gets out of balance, and we love this life too much. There are sure to be times when we simply don't want to follow Christ into the pain and suffering of taking up our own cross. This is certainly true when the cross we bear is cancer.

Jesus calls for us to hate this life and follow him to Golgotha. The cross is pain, and yet it is love. The cross is death, and yet it is life. He calls us to take up our own cross which, in no manner, precludes love and is thus the way of life. Christ the sustainer of life calls us to a balanced love for this life while preparing for a better life in Him. He calls us to follow Him, sometimes even into the midst of disease and death. Yet only as we share in his death can we in turn share in his resurrection and victory over death.

The church does so much to prepare people for life after death, but now I question if it is doing enough to prepare them for death itself and the suffering that leads up to that death. Thomas Merton writes, *"Those who love true life, therefore, frequently think about their death. Their life is full of a silence that is an anticipated victory over death. Silence, indeed, makes death our servant and even our friend."*[36] If this silent approach to death is the one generally adopted by the church, then I doubt it is by design, and I don't believe it to be in the best interest of the general church body.

Saint Paul made death a servant and even a friend, and I can't imagine him being silent for very long about anything. Paul seems to have been a communal Christian; Merton, on the other hand, was an accomplished monk and thus knew and respected silence as a potent spiritual tool. While in seminary, I was required to undergo a three day silent prayer and reflection. That exercise was introduced and monitored by faculty with much trepidation and caution, including ready access to 24/7 counseling for those who could not emotionally handle that much silence. Those students who were in any kind of crisis were exempted from that requirement and given other makeup work instead. They needed community in the midst of suffering and crisis.

Even our God is a community of three persons. So I, like Paul, am also a communal Christian who appreciates the extended body of Christ upon earth, the community of believers that is the church. I need others, I need the church, I need that body, and I need it to be vocal and reaffirming. One or more members of the body sustain the other. However, I think Merton is right-on when he articulates that those who love life frequently think about their death. If such is the case, then the church needs to address not just life after death, but the dying process itself. I am sure we all need a little silence from time to time, but we also need community. We need to huddle around the open grave and recite aloud the Lord's Prayer. The priest just cannot remain silent. He or she must cry out on behalf of all, *"All of us go down to the dust, yet even at the grave we make our song: Alleluia, alleluia, alleluia."* That acclamation is not for the deceased, the one who has already passed through the gate to eternal life. Rather, it is for those of us left standing there, staring at that grave.

There is one very helpful and even instructive line from one of the optional collects offered for use in the Book of Common Prayer's Burial of the Dead. That line reads, *"Give us faith to see in death the gate of eternal life, so that in quiet confidence we may continue our course on earth, until, by your call, we are reunited with those who have gone before; through Jesus Christ our Lord."* This uncomplicated and straightforward prayer prioritizes "faith" as the primary tool for our use in preparing for biological death. It treats death as a separate entity from eternal life; it is the gate leading to, rather than a part of, eternity. It prescribes both "quiet confidence" and merely "living our lives" as an appropriate course of action in the face of our own mortality. The prayer also reminds us that God is in control and will call us when our time arrives. It also recaps for us that we have loved ones that have already passed through that gate and are waiting for us on the other side. We not only have Christ's death to focus upon, but the deaths of all the saints and all our loved ones. I find tremendous strength in the thought that my own dad went through that gate gracefully, and thus, so can I. He was a loving and gentle man with remarkable faith in Christ. He did all within his power to pass that faith on to his children. I am most thankful for his witness for it is a tremendous help for me in facing my own death.

I suppose all of these concepts could be better and more often articulated by the church. I know that not many congregants are eager to be reminded of their own mortality. But Christ spent much of his ministry struggling to prepare his immediate followers for his death. Faith does seem to be the key factor in preparing for our own biological death. However, it is surely a special kind of faith. It must not be the faith that God is always going to intervene to perform some special and exceptional miracle in the midst of our pending death, but the faith required to live out that "quiet daily confidence" noted in the collect.

We live in a time and a culture that is very efficient at removing death and suffering from the public view. There is much the church could do to depict biological death as a crucial component of this life that, in time, validates and justifies our faith. The funeral service has been, is now, and will in all probability continue to be the primary tool the institutional church utilizes to prepare its members for their own eventual dying process. The fact that so many funerals are improperly conducted ought not to serve to dissuade the church from celebrating this ancient life-cycle observance of and from the church. And yet today there is a disturbing trend to move the funeral service from the church to the local neighborhood funeral parlor. Even more alarming is the eagerness of some of the clergy to turn the role of chief grief counselor over to the ever-caring mortician and the funeral industry. What an absolute shame! Morticians provide a valuable and even noble service. Yet they ought not to become the family pastor at the very peak crisis and loss.

With very few exceptions, we all vividly recall the first funeral we attended as children or adolescents. Most of us have carried that relatively brief but unforgettable episode in time with us through life. Whether or not we realize it, that memory and experience has played a vital role in forming our personal fears, reflections, and even beliefs and expectations about dying. Hopefully, it was a positive experience for you, with loving folks in a very familiar setting like your church or regular place of worship. Children can usually find great comfort in familiar surroundings. The mortuary chapel is a seldom to be visited structure designed solely for processing death. Children realize this. Regardless of its fine décor, it will likely not lend itself well to casting enduring and comforting memories. However, the child knows the church for the baptisms, infant dedications, confirmations, weddings, and other such grand and glorious celebrations that occur there. Grandma's casket will not seem all that foreboding as it rests near the same spot the crèche stood during last year's Christmas pageant.

Of course, parents should properly prepare their children for their first funeral experience. When a service is planned for a funeral that is expected to draw a significant number of children and young teens, consideration should be given by the clergy to inviting the parents and children to the church in advance of the service for a brief explanation of what is going to occur and what they will experience. If the priest or pastor is not especially gifted in working with children, the assistance of someone from the church who is so gifted should be solicited. Usually, a familiar and long tenured children's Sunday school teacher will be invaluable in this endeavor. The most important factor in this little pre-funeral gathering will be found in the opportunity given to the children to ask questions. I cannot overstate the importance of those questions, for their answers will be there for those youngsters sixty, seventy, or eighty years later as they face their own deaths.

A brief note found amongst the rubrics in the Book of Common Prayer's "Order for Burial" rather succinctly captures the true essence of what a Christian burial service ought to be about. It reads, *"The liturgy for the dead is an Easter liturgy. It finds all its meaning in the resurrection. Because Jesus was raised from the dead, we too, shall be raised. The liturgy therefore, is characterized by joy, in the certainty that 'neither death, nor life, nor angels, nor principalities, nor things present, nor things to come, nor powers, nor height, nor depth, nor anything else in all creation, will be able to separate us from the love of God in Christ. This joy, however, does not make human grief unchristian. The very love we have for each other in Christ brings deep sorrow when we are parted by death. Jesus himself wept at the grave of his friend. So, while we rejoice that one we love has entered into the nearer presence of our Lord, we sorrow in sympathy with those who mourn."*[37]

Most acknowledge that the funeral service is for the living rather than the deceased. The liturgical church draws upon yet another service that ministers to both the living and the dying, and it is commonly referred to as 'The Last Rites.' For many Protestants, the 'Lesser Sacrament of Extreme Unction,' or more appropriately, 'Ministration at the Time of Death,' conjures up images of the pre-reformation church and thus is not considered a viable means of comforting both the sufferer and his or her family and friends by most protestant groups. This is regrettable for the fundamental nature of this service is simply earnest and heartfelt prayer for and with a dying person. If the sufferer is capable of receiving communion, such is offered.

The Book of Common Prayer liturgy for "Ministration at the Time of Death" offers some of the most striking and evocative prayer language to be found in any form of worship. When offered faithfully, these prayers and commendations become most consoling and encouraging for all involved. Such as: *"Depart, O Christian soul, out of this world; in the Name of God the Father Almighty who created you; In the Name of Jesus Christ who redeemed you; In the Name of the Holy Spirit who sanctifies you. May your rest be this day in peace, and your dwelling place in the Paradise of God. Into your hands, O merciful Savior, we commend your servant (Name). Acknowledge, we humbly beseech you a sheep of your own fold, a lamb of your own flock, a sinner of your own redeeming. Receive him/her into the arms of your mercy, into the blessed rest of everlasting peace, and into the glorious company of the saints in light."*[38]

Then from the 'Vigil' that follows comes, *"Receive, O Lord, your servant, for he returns to you. Wash him in the holy font of everlasting life, and clothe him in his heavenly wedding garment. May she hear your words of invitation, 'Come, you blessed of my Father. May she gaze upon you, Lord, face to face, and taste the blessedness of perfect rest. May angels surround her, and saints welcome her in peace. Almighty God, our Father in heaven, before who live all who die in the Lord: Receive our brother/sister (Name) into the courts of your heavenly dwelling place. Let his heart and soul now ring out in joy to you, O Lord, the living God, and the God of those who live. This we ask through Christ our Lord. Amen"*[39]

It often seems to me that doing 'Last Rites' for someone brings Easter morning into the dead of night. Friends and family members who participate in these wonderful prayers offer the prayers on behalf of the dying loved one. However, they also carry those words in their hearts for years to come and rely upon their comforting imagery as they form their faith and their hopes and fears about their own inevitable dying process. The old phrase "blessed assurance" always seems to burst forth from the midst of those prayers designated for use in the 'Last Rites' liturgy.

Then, too, churches that no longer observe "Ash Wednesday" and the season of Lent are neglecting a most excellent means of assisting parishioners in coping with life and their own subsequent natural death. Each year, year after year, those who still observe Ash Wednesday make their way to the front of the church and kneel at the altar rail. The priest walks by, dips his or her thumb into a pot of black ashes, and traces a large and bold cross on the forehead of the believer. The priest then proclaims to the individual, "Remember that you are dust, and to dust you shall return." These sobering words remind us of our mortal nature but are uniquely presented within a worship format intended to celebrate God's gift of eternal life. Communion follows the imposition of ashes and then follows the entire season of Lent which is intended to offer a time of self-examination and repentance by prayer, fasting, and self-denial and by reading and meditating on God's holy word.[40] Those who celebrate such Lenten observances year after year grow accustomed to confronting their own mortality.

Humility and Surrender

Midway through Hezekiah's poem comes an auspicious key stanza. *"Now I walk humbly throughout my years because of this anguish I have felt. Lord your discipline is good, for it leads to life and health."* A faith that God will miraculously heal us and thus deliver us from death may be a wonderful concept and is very appropriate at times, but such a faith will not be helpful in preparing us for the eventual reality of our own demise. There is a difference between being delivered from death and being delivered by death. We delude ourselves when we assume those who have been miraculously healed have avoided death. It's only a matter of time. We know that even Lazarus eventually died a second biological death, and his body returned to the grave. Paul did have that properly directed faith when he wrote, *"So we are always confident, even though we know that as long as we live in these bodies we are not at home with the Lord. For we live by believing and not by seeing. Yes, we are fully confident, and we would rather be away from these earthly bodies, for then we would be at home with the Lord."*[41] I stand in absolute awe of Paul's emotional courage and remarkable faith.

Of course, I'm no St. Paul, so I really struggled with these matters. Hezekiah's similar struggle is reflected in the words of his poetry. *"I waited patiently all night, but I was torn apart as though by lions. Delirious, I chattered like a swallow or a crane, and then I moaned like a mourning dove. My eyes grew tired of looking to heaven for help. I am in trouble, Lord. Help me.*"[42] I now understand Hezekiah. I've been there. I had to go there to get to the truth of the matter. I had to go there to truly understand that I must trust God completely. I couldn't manipulate or even help facilitate death or even my fear of death. Waiting for God ought to be championed as a viable factor in merely living a fulfilling life. Waiting for God is an act of both humility and surrender. However, it is not a surrender of stifled resignation but one of great hope and expectation. After all, we are waiting for something that we expect to arrive. We are waiting for God!

I wanted to go find God, but I couldn't, so I just gave up and prayed, "Lord, I can't do this; you have to do it for me. You must come to me; I'll just be sitting here in my favorite chair waiting for you." My simple prayer continued, "I'm not God – you are, so be God. Do your thing; I'll be here waiting." There have been far more eloquent prayers to emerge from my lips, but never a more earnest prayer. Isaiah prayed this same prayer as it should be prayed: *"Oh, that you would rend the heavens and come down, that the mountains would tremble before you! As when the fire sets twigs ablaze and causes water to boil, come down to make your name known to your enemies and cause the nations to quake before you! For when you did awesome things that we did not expect, you came down, and the mountains trembled before you. Since ancient times, no one has heard, no ear perceived, no eye has seen any God besides you, who acts on behalf of those who wait for Him."*[43]

Could it be that simply waiting for God is our best means of preparing for biological death? Waiting takes faith! However, sometimes waiting is easier said than done as our own impatience can get in the way even in our personal preparation for death. Just as I was so impatient with the doctors, I was equally impatient with God. Waiting for God is not a natural or comfortable thing for many of us to do.

I have the bad habit of asking God for something, and then rather than patiently waiting for God to act, I set out to help God give it to me just the way I want it. This is not merely impatience as much as it is a "control thing." It seems to me that if I can help, then perhaps I can be in at least partial control, and thus I am more likely to end up with what I want, how I want it, and when I want it. Probably, God does want me to do my part, but perhaps I sometimes try to do part of God's work as well. Of course, the obvious result of this over-done, self-help approach is that I seldom really know if God actually provides or if I've simply manipulated what I wanted all along. True to form, I tried this with my fear of a pre-mature death and ran head-on into a brick wall. I found that this does not work in preparing to die. Death ultimately forces surrender of all control in favor of total trust in God. We must simply wait in faith for God to act.

Earlier, I wrote of my blind dog Talbot's craving for self-reliance and independence as demonstrated in his desire to run free. I suspect common impatience is a key component of that longing. He knows he needs me but senses I slow him down. They say a dog takes on the characteristics of his master. I guess Talbot is a lot like me, or perhaps I'm like Talbot. I'm often just too impatient to wait for God and too spiritually blind to take my own walk through life. Consequently, I found myself running not only in emotional circles, but also in intellectual and theological circles when first confronted with cancer and the very real possibility of an early death. Only when I realized I was going nowhere with my own intellect did I eventually just give up and wait for God. My lack of control was humbling, but I knew I was surrendering to a mighty God.

Waiting for God was ultimately all I could do. In so doing, I relinquished all control, and as I waited, an awareness of a deep abiding peace and comfort filled me. It surprised me. It was unexpected and seemed pleasantly awkward.

That overwhelming spiritual awareness didn't come from my intellect or emotions. It wasn't a feeling. It was real. It defies description far beyond my ability to put it in plain words. The best means I have of expressing it is to simply say that it was a body and mind permeating discernment or reassurance that, as in God's image, my life, too, is eternal. I believe I was created in God's image, and in that image is the "eternal."

It is love, and it is about time. The 5th chapter of John's Gospel cites Christ, "Very truly I tell you, the Son can do nothing on his own, but only what he sees the Father doing; for whatever the Father does, the Son does likewise." I am confident that even as a young boy, Jesus saw God's miracle in the natural process of turning water into wine, so he launched his earthly ministry by doing the same at that wedding in Cana of Galilee. As a teenager, even I saw God performing that miracle with my own eyes. Now before you begin to think I'm losing my mind, let me explain that at that time I was living in Linden, California, and on a clear day I could see the snow on the high peaks of the Sierra Nevada Mountains from our house. Then, during the spring/summer thaw, I saw that water gushing down off those mountains and pushing back the banks of the diverting canals that criss-crossed the central valley. I saw the grape growers around Lodi irrigating their vineyards with that water. Then I saw, and even worked in the harvest as we cut ripe grapes bursting with juice which was water on its way to becoming wine. Then, later as I would pass the wineries, I could smell the water-turned-grape-juice turning into wine. Ventnor's don't manufacture wine. Like the servants at the wedding, they assist God. Mary told the wedding servants, "Do whatever he tells you." She knew more than others that God provided the creation, the power, and the time; God does all the work.

We read the Gospel account of the miracle of the feeding of the multitude from five barley loaves and two fish, and we are reminded that God supplies the creation, power, and time. Just give me two fish, assuming they are male and female, and the barley grain it took to make those five loaves, and give me an Iowa farm with a nice sized pond, and most importantly, give me enough time, and I, too, will feed five thousand people from those original two fish & that handful of barley grain. That's nature. That's God's miracle that surrounds us with those miracles we so often just take for granted. Jesus simply does in five minutes what it usually takes God years to do naturally in His creation. You see, it's all about time or, more specifically, about power over time. You and I have no power over time. But God is bigger than the down-to-earth concept of time he created for us. Christ, as God incarnate, has and uses that power.

In John's Gospel, he is quoted as saying, *"Very truly I tell you, before Abraham was, I am."*[44] He didn't say that he was before Abraham. He said I am (present tense) before Abraham was (past tense). He comes not from history, even though he became a part of human history, he comes from a dimension above time. He comes to us from the eternal now; eternity in the present tense.

John's Gospel story about feeding of the multitude also cites the miracle of Christ walking on water. Now here's a seemingly flamboyant attention-grabbing stunt that stretches our faith and our imaginations. Miraculously healing the sick or feeding the hungry makes sense to us. But why would he do something so seemingly sleight-of-hand or slight of feet as walking on water? Why would he perform a miracle like that? Was He just showing off? What purpose did it serve? Who did that help?

Well, to better understand the miracle of walking on the water, we must get into God's time machine we call Holy Scripture and go back to the very beginning of "time," back to the genesis. *"And the earth was without form and void; and darkness was upon the face of the deep. And the spirit of*

God moved upon the face of the waters."[45] Jesus walking on the Sea of Galilee was not the first time God had walked on water. God was moving across the face of the waters before time existed. But that is past and because the concept of "the past" is part of our concept of God-created time, even in his incarnate form, he was still the master of time. *"Then they wanted to take him into the boat, and immediately the boat reached the land toward which they were travelling."* What Hollywood pop culture might call a time warp is just God being God.

We dare not separate and divide the members of the trinity. The Son - that humble and gentle man named Jesus, our friend, has the power to do as the Father does. He, too, has the power to work miracles, the power to move across the face of the waters, the power to transcend time. His power and control over time is awesome. It is astonishing. His disciples were terrified to see God moving across the face of the waters, but Jesus said to them as Jesus says to us today, "It is I; do not be afraid." Do not be afraid of time and/ or the ravages of time. The master of time is with us even as we face a disease like cancer.

We ask a most important question about the miraculous feeding of the multitude. Just what does this miracle say to us today in the midst of our suffering? I believe it speaks to us about Christ's right use of power over time for nurturing, healing, delivering, freeing, and loving us. God uses power for life. In his book, "The Eternal Now, theologian Paul Tillich writes, *"We speak of time in three ways or modes – the past, the present and the future. Every child is aware of them, but no wise person has ever penetrated their mystery. We become aware of them when we hear a voice telling us, "You will come to an end." Our awareness of time begins with the anxious anticipation of the end."*[46] I agree, but with faith in an eternal God who exercises power over time, we hope and pray Christ will use that power to enable us to survive time despite natural death. In fact, through faith, through prayer, through His word, through the Sacraments, through Christ, I think we spiritually already have one foot in that eternal now.

Tillich also writes, *"There is one power that surpasses the all consuming power of time – that is the eternal. He who was and is, and is to come, the beginning and the end. He gives us forgiveness for what has passed. He gives us courage for what is to come. He gives us rest in his eternal presence."*[47] As believers, nothing can separate us from that eternal presence.

There is love in His presence and peace even in the midst of life's storms. The winds were strong, the waves were high, the water was pouring into the hull, and the boat was definitely going down. But Jesus was asleep in the back of the boat. So the disciples did what I would do; they woke him up. Then they asked, *"Lord, don't you even care?"* "We are dying here Lord; don't you care?" Jesus must have been momentarily startled; probably not by the storm or by the sinking boat, but by the fact that his small band of friends had apparently lost faith. They apparently hadn't lost faith in his ability to do miracles; rather, they seemed to have lost faith in his love for them. "Don't you care, Lord?" Centuries earlier, King Hezekiah was dying, and he pled, *"I'm in trouble, Lord. Help me!"* Here, the disciples were in trouble, but their first inclination was not to ask for help, but to question the Master's love for them. "Don't you care?"

Maybe I am just playing word games, for we know that those disciples knew that if Christ really cared for them, then surely he would help them. Surely he would rescue them. But they were panic stricken; they were on the way to the deep, well on their way to death, and I don't think they were carefully considering, weighing, and selecting their words. I think they shouted out their first concern, and those instinctive words accurately betrayed their real lack of faith. They had witnessed the miracles, they knew Christ could do marvelous super-natural things, but the question must have lingered in their individual and collective minds and souls. Could he care about them; could he love them such as they were? I think that was the real disturbance, that was the more threatening storm, and that required the greater miracle.

We know Jesus knew and often quoted the Psalms. He doubtlessly knew and was familiar with the lines, "*Then they cried to the Lord in their trouble, and he brought them out of their distress; he made the storm be still, and the waves of the sea were hushed. Then they were glad because they had quiet, and he brought them to their desired heaven. Let them thank the Lord for his steadfast love.*"[48] He knew those lines, and he knew my favorite line from the 46th Psalm. It says the same thing but is a lot more direct and to the point; it simply reads: "*Be still and know that I am God!*" That line is one of my very favorite passages from all of Holy Scripture. Be still and know that I am God!

Anyone with a cancer diagnosis is surely no stranger to emotional storms. We know emotional lightning and thunder; we experience strong winds, hail, and heavy rain. Nor are we strangers to spiritual storms. As with non-sufferers, common guilt can so easily turn our hearts to distress. We all know we have sinned, we know those disgusting deeds, and we know that God knows. It would surely take a miracle for God to love us after what we've done. Thus we sail into those guilt-ridden spiritual storms and we fear, battle, and struggle with them even in the midst of our seemingly unrelated battle with cancer. Christ may seem to be asleep at the back of our boat. But the Holy Comforter never sleeps. That's part of what Christ meant when he proclaimed. "*It is to your advantage that I go away, for if I do not go away the Holy Comforter will not come to you; but if I go, I will send him to you.*"[49]

That guilt and doubt doesn't come from God. We know better than to dwell upon such, but we do, and thus we often conjure up our own worse storms. We either don't know how, or we forget and neglect to love ourselves, and so it seems impossible that a holy, pure, and righteous God would love us. We sometimes refuse to forgive ourselves and wrestle with those storms even in the midst of our physical suffering, and we long for Christ to simply stand up and say, "Peace be still."

We may never go out to sea, but each of us is sure to sail into storms in this life. Some experience more violent and tragic storms than others do. In his book, "The Perfect Storm," Sebastion Junger writes of rogue waves out in the Atlantic as high as 90 feet. That is awesome. But to the cancer sufferer, such can surely seem mild compared to some of the spiritual, emotional, and certainly physical storms some have weathered. Our lives are pushed violently over on their sides, and we hold on and shout out, "Lord, don't you even care?" We need that incarnate deity, we need that savior who has experienced what we experience, and we need the Master to raise his hand and say to the storm, "Peace, be still." Reason will tell us that not every storm will stop instantaneously, but our faith assures us the Master cares. There, in the midst of the storm, we encounter the eternal God, our personal friend who knows us, forgives us, loves us, and gives us peace. We only trust in He who cares for us and about us. There, in the midst of our humble surrender, we encounter the eternal and find peace.

Faith and Rescue

Surrender not only leads to peace, but to change as well. King Hezekiah was greatly changed in his suffering and ultimate healing. One might say he became a different person. I would suggest that rather than becoming a different person, he became a new person, almost like a rebirth. At least, that was what I experienced. I was still me, but I emerged from my encounter with that apparent eminent end of life and simultaneous encounter with God to assume a fresh new mindset and spirituality. In my encounter and in my surrender, I was greatly changed.

Yet we dare never champion this process of positive change as an indicator of pre-eminence. Those who suffer are in no way spiritually superior to those who don't suffer. Such arrogance will only lead to the travesty, if not heresy, of celebrating pain for pain sake. As King Hezekiah wrote, "Yes, this anguish was good for me, for you have rescued me." Likewise, in our own surrender, suffering, and encounter, we can share a unified belief with others absent a uniformed experience. God does not clone believers. Perhaps for me it was simply a matter of needing to learn things the "hard way;" then again, perhaps it was something far more unique and mystical.

In his classic work "*I and Thou,*" twentieth-century Jewish theologian Martin Buber writes much of human encounter with the eternal. I cite the following excerpts:

"What is it that is eternal: the primal phenomenon,

present in the here and now, of what we call revelation? It is man's emerging from the moment of the supreme encounter, being no longer the same as when entering into it. The moment of encounter is not a 'living experience' that stirs in the receptive soul and blissfully rounds itself out: (rather) something happens to man. At times it is like feeling a breath and at times like a wrestling match; no matter: something happens. Actually we receive what we did not have before, in such a manner that we know it has been given to us. In the language of the Bible: 'Those who wait for God will receive strength in exchange.' Man receives and what he receives is not a 'content', but a presence, a presence as strength. You do not know how to point to or define the meaning, you lack any formula or image for it, and yet it is more certain for you than the sensation of your senses. It is not the meaning of 'another life' but that of this our life, not that of a 'beyond' but of this our world, and it wants to be demonstrated by us in this life and this world."[50]

Although Buber maintains, we lack the ability to interpret it. I'll hazard a partial and even shallow explanation as it is specifically relevant to my case and say I suspect for the very first time in my life, I recognized my soul taking the lead primarily on its own. I suspect I recognized my soul functioning not in total sync with my mind and body. It was my spirit in God's spirit manifesting its own eternal nature. It is surely God's will for our soul, mind, and body to be balanced and synchronized in great harmony and in unison. However, we expect the soul to live forever even while we recognize the inevitability of eventual biological death. Thus it stands to reason that some day there must be a separation. So perhaps, just perhaps, true preparation for death requires faithfully waiting for that God orchestrated discernment of at least the faintest ascendancy of our soul over our minds and bodies. I think I found that when the body and mind loosen their grip, the soul is prepared to take charge, to carry on.

As a young police officer, I once had to climb a ninety-foot fire truck ladder up the side of a tall building. I don't like heights, and I could feel my grip tighten on the rungs of that ladder as I neared the top. In my high anxiety, each rung higher seemed to require just a little tighter grip. As I reached the top, I had to swing out over the side of the ladder and plant my feet and body weight on the safety of the flat roof. I did so but then found it very difficult to let go of the ladder. I was safely on the roof; I no longer needed the ladder, but it was as though my hands had a mind of their own and just didn't want to release their grip. I think that is about as far as I progressed in this spiritual discernment about death. It was not God's time for me to let go of this life. It was incomplete; I was standing there with my feet firmly planted on the safe roof, clinging to that ladder. This time, I climbed back down. But now I am at least confident that when God's time does come, I will be able to let go of the ladder.

I know this discernment of the eternal within me was not a mere emotion or feeling because it ran directly contrary to my ongoing troubled thought process. My thought process was surprised and interrupted. I mentally asked myself, "Where did that come from?" I was spiritually greatly comforted in the midst of emotional worries about the possibility of dying.

My spirituality temporarily out-paced my intellect. I doubted our intellect alone ever really reaches the point of true emotional preparation for death. My ailing ninety-year old mother put it simply; "No one ever really wants to die." In fact, in the midst of that spiritual blessed assurance of eternal life, I had a sense of guilt over my insight that biological death was no longer my primary concern. I sensed that I was somehow shirking my duty as a human being to hang onto life at absolutely all costs. I felt I owed it to my loved ones to fight biological death to the bitter end, even while my creator was assuring me that my eventual end would not be bitter.

In time, subsequent surgeries, suffering, and weariness were to exert great impact upon this line of thinking as I personally came to an eventual point when I truly wanted to die. My mother was wrong; people do come to a place in life when and where biological death offers a blessed healing. But that was not part of Hezekiah's experience, or part of my Hezekiah experience. That all was yet to come in God's own time.

We are an impatient people. However much we may deny it, the timing of working through these matters is certainly in God's hands. Thus, as Martin Buber asserts, my experience was not the meaning of "another life" but that of this my life, not that of a "beyond" but of this our world, and it wants to be demonstrated by me in this life and this world. I've thought about and now written about the church and its role in our preparation for dying. Of course, the church is not the building or even the institution; it is every believer, and it is me. We are one body. Thus, we are not alone in our living, and we are not alone in our dying.

As you might expect, I found that preparation for death is not a solitary process. Loved ones are there in the very middle of that painful path, and I was astounded by the fact that almost all the pain in preparing for death emanates from love; hence the temptation to outwardly deny suffering and feign courage. We want to spare those we love. Loved ones suffer as much or more than those dying. But then awareness of their suffering adds more pain to the dying. It is true; we suffer because we love. My father-in-law died suffering from prostate cancer in the mid nineteen-seventies. That was prior to the many treatment and care advances and options available today, and so his suffering was lengthy and intense. The whole extended family suffered with him because of our love for this man. He was suffering, therefore we were suffering.

Telling my wife and children that I was diagnosed with Renal Cell Carcinoma was one of the most painful things I have ever had to do in my life. Knowing the risks of major surgery with a low-blood-platelet count made it painful to embrace my dear wife in that chaotic hospital corridor early that morning just before I walked into the surgical prep room. I had good reason to consider the possibility that it would be our last embrace, and I knew she knew. I walked away from her that morning with a lump in my throat, vowing that if I survived, I would never again take a hug for granted. If I didn't love my wife and children, and they didn't love me, it wouldn't hurt so much.

C. S. Lewis writes, *"To love at all is to be vulnerable. Love anything and your heart will certainly be wrung and possibly broken. If you want to make sure of keeping intact, you must give your love to no one, not even an animal. Wrap it up carefully round with hobbies and little luxuries; avoid all entanglements; lock it up safe in the casket or coffin of your selfishness. But in that casket – safe, dark, motionless, airless – it will change. It will not be broken; it will become unbreakable, impenetrable, irredeemable. The alternative to tragedy, or at least the risk of tragedy, is damnation. The only place outside heaven where you can be perfectly safe from all the dangers of love is hell."*[51] Of course, Lewis himself did not personally escape the painful dangers of love. We can feel his suffering in the words he wrote concerning the death of his wife. *"I look up at the night sky. Is anything more certain than that in all those vast times and spaces, if I were allowed to search them, I should nowhere find her face, her voice, her touch? She died. She is dead. Is the word so difficult to learn?"*[52]

During seminary, I had inadequately studied Kazoh Kitamori's 'Pain of God Theology' and had not previously personally grasped his concept of love rooted in the pain of God. I do now! Now I understand how this pain of mine could only be healed and made meaningful as it unites with the pain God suffered in the crucifixion of his own dear son.

I discovered that my pain took on meaning as it conveyed to me a sense of God's pain. From my own pain came a deeper understanding of God. I think Kitamori was correct in at least his assertion that the bridge between God and humanity is pain. The platonic philosophical concept of an apathetic, pleased, and satisfied God governing in the midst of my pain not only does not make sense to me, it seems quite contrary to the essential gospel message. That is Christ suffering on the cross was both truly human and truly God.

Kitamori, who was a 1950s and 60s Professor of Systematic Theology at Tokyo Union Theological Seminary, found God's pain in God's internal conflict between his wrath and his love. *"What sola fide was to Luther, "The love rooted in the pain of God" is to Kitamori. The theology of the pain of God describes the heart of God most deeply......"*[53] As a graduate of Japan Lutheran Theological Seminary, he was greatly influenced by the theology of Martin Luther who had explained this same concept as "God fighting with God – one God." Thus, God suffers a troubled heart as he justifiably rejects me in my sinfulness and yet embraces me in his love.

It is against the very essence of "holy" to tolerate evil, yet the essence of holy love is to embrace unconditionally. That presents a painful conflict. It is against the very essence of God-given life to tolerate death. True enough, in nature, all that lives eventually dies. But that death-inevitable nature was created by and resides within the nature of God which is eternal. Humanity was created in the image of the eternal. Humankind is destined to die a natural biological death. Yet through spiritual rebirth, we shall live on for all eternity in our eternal creator.

Spiritual birth, like its bodily counterpart, is painful. This conflict between life and death could only be resolved and rectified through the pain of Golgotha. As Trinitarian believers, we cannot separate the vicarious pain of the Father from the pain of the Son on the cross. It was sixth century

North African monk and Bishop Fabius Fulgentia who wrote of the Trinity, *"Because the persons are not separate things, they do not do things separately, and they do not do different things. All the works of God are works of the Father done in the Son and perfected through the Spirit."*[54] The members of the Trinity cannot be separated any more than they can be denied their individuality. They are not separate things; they weren't separate on the cross, and they weren't separate on Pentecost. Practically any parent who has ever had a child suffer understands that God the Father suffers vicariously because God loves. We see this theme very appropriately carried into our own relationships with others, especially those closest to us. We see God's love carried into our own suffering. It is only through our own suffering that we can begin to understand God's suffering and thus, God's love. We see God's love carried into the suffering of our loved ones. God's love-borne ability to suffer with us enables us to suffer with others.

Professor Kitamori cites Hezekiah's friend Isaiah (63:15) and the Prophet Jeremiah (31:20) by way of substantiating his theology of love rooted in God's Pain. He exegetes the Hebrew verb 'hamah' found in both passages as inter-changeably and/or simultaneously meaning God's love and God's pain. I leave the language exegesis to the scholars, but Kitamori carries his interpretation beyond mere word play. He writes, *"The word 'hamah' meaning simultaneously both pain and love, is not simply a mystery of language, but also a mystery of grace. That is, the mystery of grace means that Christ of the cross is at the same time Christ of the resurrection....."*[55]

Thus, Kitamori's words are as close as I can come to understanding the implications of my belief in eternal life in the face of my fear and suffering. It is a mystery of grace! My suffering has no eternal earning or bartering power or value in and of itself because I am mere creature, not the creator of life. God created life, and thus God's suffering has all the clout. He was at the same time both truly human and truly God. He is at the same time both the sufferer of the cross and the victor of the resurrection. Because he loves me, he suffers for me, and that love and suffering – his love and his suffering - includes me and is sufficient to merit eternity for me. Through love, my pain becomes part of his pain, my death becomes part of his death, and thus, his victory over death also becomes my victory.

In a more practical manner, Kitamori also draws upon both the Old Testament story of Abraham on Mount Moriah and Christ's story of the prodigal son as analogies of God's love for us rooted in his pain. The prodigal always causes the parent much pain and suffering, but in no manner deters the parent's love if that love is unconditional in nature. To continue the love requires the parent to embrace the pain. Not merely the pain inflicted by the rebellious child against the parent, but vicariously the pain ultimately experienced by the child as a natural result of that rebelliousness. Again, only in God's love could I find meaning to all that was happening to me. This all took a little time, a few tears, some reading and reflection, and a lot of prayer, and still the outcome was a mystery of God's grace. As previously noted, Saint Paul wrote, *"For now we see through a glass darkly..."*

Kitamori writes, *"We cannot know directly what the pain of God is; we can only know it through our own pain. Our pain must witness to the pain of God by becoming the symbol of the pain of God."*[56] Our pain can only have meaning as it witnesses to God's pain.

Thus, I began to mentally and spiritually reflect upon, explore, and adjust to the unexpected news of a serious life-threatening malady. I know St. Paul would caution me "to be not anxious about anything, but in everything, by prayer and petition with thanksgiving present my requests to God." I seem to have mastered the latter part of that warning far better than the first part. I know how to pray and petition and make my requests known to God. But all too often my prayers are motivated by anxiety. When it comes to the avoidance of all anxiety, I must rely upon Paul's earlier comments from that same letter. Paul earlier writes concerning God carrying through to completion a good work He has begun in us. As I have already noted, I've never known a person who didn't experience some degree of worry or anxiety from time to time; perhaps we're all works in progress. I worried, I prayed, I trusted God and only then did I begin to see the ordeal as a growth and strengthening process.

I met with my new doctor at the pharmacy on that Saturday and was then in his office first thing Tuesday morning with my CT Scan images in hand. He carefully scrutinized them, shook his head, and said, "This is big and ugly."

I questioned, "So it has metastasized?"

He quickly answered, "No, I don't think so; of course only God knows for sure, but I can't see any sign that it has spread beyond the right kidney. We will know more after surgery." He also told me the left kidney appeared normal and healthy.

Tears came to my eyes as I breathed a deep sigh of relief and asked for confirmation, "So this means it is curable?"

The doctor answered, "These are very good pictures, and they indicate this should be very curable." He added, "Of course, these don't give us a great view of the bladder."

I asked, "Are you going to look in there today?" While reluctant because I knew what all that entailed, I was none-the-less willing to endure the discomfort.

To my pleasant surprise, he answered, "No, I'm going to have you on the operating table in a few days. I'll take a close look then. I won't find anything I'm not prepared to handle at that time. We will spare you some discomfort today."

That response made a lot of sense and caused me to

consider the approach of my first doctor. We hear so much about unnecessary procedures that only serve to drive up the costs. I am confident such was not the case with the first doctor who demonstrated caring caution. Needless tests just didn't correlate with his busy schedule. It seems to me the last thing he would want for his schedule would be just one more test. Did his interest in a pre-surgical look in the bladder indicate a lengthy wait for surgery? I doubt that it merely indicated a lack of concern for my comfort. Was it merely the result of office procedural bureaucracy or was it some insurance requirement based upon liability issues? I will never know. However, I did pause to appreciate my decision to seek a second opinion and my decision to go with a doctor who at least seemed to demonstrate greater compassion. I am confident others might prefer my first doctor over the one I ultimately selected to do my surgery. We all have different personal preferences, different likes and dislikes. However, I can't imagine anyone questioning the wisdom of seeking a second opinion.

In his office that day, my surgeon diagnosed my illness as Renal Cell Carcinoma and explained that it could be any one of four different strains or types. He explained that some are very aggressive and fast acting and others are relatively slow. He further clarified that post-surgery pathology would show the specific type. I asked, "So can I tell people that I have cancer?" He replied, "Yes, it is cancer." In an odd sort of way, even that seemed somehow comforting. That early big unknown had dissipated. Now, at least I knew. I now knew what to pray for and how to pray. With the doctor's skill and compassion and the certain knowledge of what I was up against, even the superficial emotional fear seemed to subside a little. I now knew the nature of the fight that awaited me.

As a priest and believer in Christ, it should surprise no one that I believe God is still capable to this day of divine intervention and "New Testament type" miraculous healing. I understand that "God's will" and "God's timing" will always take precedence in such matters and that I may not always receive the specific type of healing I request when and how I request it. Nonetheless, I believe in divine healing.

It should not astound anyone that from the very first hint that I was suffering some sort of illness, my prayers were in petition for such healing. What may amaze some is the fact that not all Christians believe in miracle healings. Christian author John Spong writes, *"I do not believe that this Jesus could or did in any literal way raise the dead, overcome a medically diagnosed paralysis, or restore sight to a person born blind or to the one in whom the ability to see had been physiologically destroyed. Nor do I believe he enabled one who is mute and profoundly deaf since birth to hear. Healing stories can be looked at in a number of ways. To view them as supernatural, miraculous events is, in my opinion, the least credible of those possibilities."*[57] At times apparent disbelief can be ever bit as amazing as miracle healings themselves.

Spong has cited what he calls his recurring theme, *"The heart cannot worship what the mind rejects."*[58] In my opinion, he has that basic tenet of faith exactly and precisely backwards. Centuries earlier, Anselm of Canterbury had it right when he said, "For I do not seek to understand in order to believe, but I believe in order to understand. For this too I believe, that 'unless I believe, I shall not understand." Anselm added, "Faith seeks understanding."[59] In his theology, John Spong seems to me to place his mind out in front of his heart to serve as sort of a filter or safety screen. If I did that with my mind, such as it is, I know that not every good thing God has for me would get through my limited and mortal intellectual mind to my unlimited and spiritually eternal heart or soul.

I do use my mind. God gave me a mind and expects me to use it to analyze life. I can even use it to be critical in my assessment of Spong's writing and personally accept or reject such. However, when I think about my life in relationship with God, I come to the reasoned conclusion that there is more going on than I can rationalize or, through intellect alone, master or even begin to comprehend. Peter J. Gomes preaches, *"We can do nothing less than affirm, and indeed confess, how great is the mystery of our religion." "To the question, 'Is the Christian faith reasonable?' the answer must be no. That is not to say that there is no reason in Christianity, which is a different matter, but it is to say that by the measure of reasonable understanding faith is not reasonable, and if that makes you uncomfortable, that is the way it is supposed to be."*[60]

We do live in the Information Age, and I think there is a great temptation to make "knowledge and reason" our God. But God is **not** knowledge – God is love. Human intellect is too fragile and ephemeral for God to be knowledge. Love is hard-wearing and resilient. God-given human love is a survivor.

God is love. Can you imagine the spiritual chaos we would face if God were knowledge and understanding? How spiritual one is, how close to God one could draw, would depend upon how bright and educated that person is. Tiny babies, who are not known for their reasoned grasp of this post-Newtonian age, are wonderfully capable of giving and receiving love. Who could be closer to God than an infant? I don't really want my relationship with God to depend so much upon my intellectual understanding of that relationship, upon how clear I think? Sometimes sailing into a storm causes us to lose our ability to think so clear. My dad was a very wise thinker, and then he suffered a massive stroke. That stroke had a negative impact upon his intellect, but it in no way negatively impacted his relationship with a God who is love. Paul writes, "Knowledge will pass away, love endures forever." I find faith in that love.

The endless cycle of idea and action,
Endless invention, endless experiment,
Brings knowledge of motion, but not of stillness,
Knowledge of speech, but not of silence;
Knowledge of words, and ignorance of the Word.
All of our knowledge brings us nearer to our ignorance.
T.S. Eliot [61]

'Faith <u>in</u> Love,' and 'faith <u>and</u> love' carried me through that summer. I am thankful for my intellect, but I found it insufficient to reason my way through this ordeal. With less than a two-week wait, I was spared a long, grueling, fearful period of anticipation in slow-motion leading up to surgery. It was Friday morning before I knew it and my wife and adult children were there, church folks, the Bishop, good friends, and fellow priests were there to pray for me and sit with my family. My elderly mother was praying in California. Folks, some of whom I didn't even know, were praying for me in about a dozen different states. Of course, those five hours of surgery were far more difficult for my family than they were for me. They were difficult for the doctor who was working on a friend, and there were some difficult times for him as my blood platelet count dropped, placing me at great risk. A low-platelet count presents difficulty in the control of bleeding.

The wounded surgeon plies the steel
That questions the distempered part;
Beneath the bleeding hands we feel
The sharp compassion of the healer's art
Resolving the enigma of the fever chart.
T.S. Eliot [62]

Just prior to surgery, a very special priest friend came into the prep room, anointed me with oil, and prayed for me.

Of course, I had done this myself for others, but I had no idea just how comforting it was to be on the receiving end of this ancient ritual just prior to such a traumatic event. I carried that blessing into the operating room, and I carried it with me into a deep sleep. Then it was Saturday morning before I knew it and the surgery was behind me. Jeff had taken out one of my kidneys, but as he explained, it hadn't been functional for quite some time anyway. I rationalized the missing organ in my realization that I had lived sixty years with just one brain, one heart, one liver, and one pancreas. And while I really appreciated the spare kidney I, like a lot of good folks, would do just fine with only one kidney. It is surprising what little affect the loss of one kidney has on one's health. All things considered, for me the surgery was the least difficult phase of my illness. Nonetheless, I was sure glad to have it behind me. When I came out from under anesthesia, my doctor was there beside my bed to tell me he believed he had gotten it all. I was then too happy to hurt too much.

My recovery was quite tolerable. I must say the pain was very adequately managed as I moved to over-the counter Tylenol shortly after my discharge from the hospital five days after surgery. I was off even Tylenol by the second week. Just as one would suspect, the hospital nursing staff had presented the full breadth of care and compassion. At one extreme were two nurses who could have been angels for all I know. At the opposite end stood a nurse who was no angel and left me with the impression that she was working long hours and was most interested in "getting out of there" at the end of her shift. People like her always cause me to reflect upon why some seem to find their way into caring, nurturing professions for which they seem so ill suited. Did she begin her career with noble compassion only to have something happen to destroy her love for those who suffer? Has she seen such extreme suffering that those who suffer less no longer merit her concern? Have some of those who suffer, abused or otherwise, offended her?

Health care, education, the justice system, the clergy, and the other caring professions each have their own small allotment of mean and/or uncaring practitioners. Their lives must be truly miserable as they minister misery to others. Years ago, my dad walked into a hospital emergency room having just suffered his third heart attack. The receptionist handed him a clip board with a lengthy bureaucratic admission form to be filled out. He started to hand it to my mother when the receptionist sternly intervened, "No, you fill it out yourself. You're not going to die." He was dead in less than thirty minutes.

My dad was a sweet gentle man, and he deserved a better love than that hospital had to offer. God help me to someday forgive that woman I've never even met! Such arrogant and cruel folks certainly remind us of our need to forgive others which can be very difficult indeed. Meanwhile, we cannot let the hurtful work done by those few overshadow the heroic service of those we might justifiably mistake for angels.

Health care providers are called to the grandest of callings which has long stood as humankind's best possible answer to Cain's question, "Am I my brother's keeper?" Indeed, they are their brother's and sister's keepers as evidenced by their work, dedication, and presence. My hospital stay confirmed one great lesson taught to me in seminary. I had entered seminary with the naïve expectation that I would learn the verbal formula for comforting the frightened sufferer and/or the devastated bereaved. I thought that, as a priest, I would go out armed with just the right strategic passages derived from Holy Scripture and the most effective things to say to bring comfort and God's blessing.

As a police officer, I always knew that I didn't have the best words for those in need of spiritual and emotional care. All I could really do was to stand by and remain with the hurting person until competent professional care could arrive, usually in the form of a priest or minister. Then in seminary, I learned that there are no magic words or rituals in a caring pastor's tool kit. When everything is said and done, it is simply his or her prayers and mere presence that makes the difference. Although reluctant at first, I think I eventually recognized and even applied this crucial teaching, but until this illness, I don't think I truly valued the spiritual significance and merit of meager human presence.

Of course, this concept goes far beyond pastoral care to encompass the concept of community itself. However, I think suffering requires more than just the knowledge of community; it cries out for the presence of community; community that the sufferer can reach out and touch. We shouldn't be too astounded by this need, for mere human presence is the holy foundation of God's own incarnation. God took on human form just to be with us. Thus, the hunger and driven quest for God's presence causes me at times to read scripture not for the information and guidance it offers, but for the discernment of the presence of a living God to be found there between the lines and amongst the words. Can you feel the presence of a compassionate and wounded God in His words according to Hosea? *"How can I give you up, Ephraim? How can I hand you over O Israel? How can I make you like Admah? How can I treat you like Zeboiim? My heart recoils within me; my compassion grows warm and tender. I will not execute my fierce anger; I will not again destroy Ephraim; for I am God and no mortal, the holy one in your midst, and I will not come in wrath."*[63]

When we suffer, we find a need for both divine community and human community, and we need both of these to be present for us in our pain. I realize we believe in an unseen God that must be worshipped in faith, but in the King James wording, God does send us the Holy Comforter. When the two meld together, that is the Holy Comforter and human community, when we can feel the presence of God in the presence of others, we are greatly comforted.

Still "just being there" sounds like such a cop-out when taken against the backdrop of our good old American work ethic. Many of us are so inculcated with the concepts of production and performance that we can grow to place such a very low value upon whom we are, absent that proficient self-propelled labor of ours. What we "do" becomes more important than "who" we are. Our production becomes our idol, and ultimately mere presence is left behind in the spiritual dust as our life becomes one giant production machine lumbering awkwardly along toward eternity.

On several occasions during my post surgical hospital stay, I awoke in the darkness of the night, drugged, confused, and frightened only to hear the sound of my thirty-four year old son asleep in the chair beside my bed. During those moments, all his life's accomplishments mattered not in the least. What mattered was that he was there with me, and thus I was spared the want to cry out, "My God, My God why have thou forsaken me?" In reflecting upon Christ's abandonment upon the cross and in my son's presence, I found God's presence and love to be very real for me. I found that holy presence in my smiling, loving daughter who was there for me throughout the day and during the evenings, and I found God in the love and patience of my devoted wife. I found that presence in the priests who came to visit and bring me Holy Eucharist. I found that presence in friends who were there for me, I found it in those who were praying for me, and I even found it in the get-well cards sent by those who couldn't visit.

The pathology analysis was due in nine days at the most. Thus, nine days after surgery, Judy and I were seated in the doctor's office, anxiously awaiting the results that would indicate so much about my future battle with cancer and give some perspective as to my chances for survival. I took great comfort in the sheer number of persons praying for good results. That bolstered my faith, and I really expected good news all along. The doctor entered the examining room and apologetically explained that the pathology results had yet to return. Of course, we were very disappointed. Others were praying and wanted to know the results, and they would be disappointed as well. The doctor promised to check out the delay and let us know just as soon as the results were available. He understood our frustration. Then the physician's assistant came in and removed the twenty-three wire staples from my abdominal incision. That pain was clearly nothing contrasted to that found in my disappointment over the delayed reports and the continued suspense.

At "surgery-plus-fifteen days," my patience was wearing thin and the doctor realized he had to give us some information. Over the phone, he cautioned me not to get my hopes up and explained the initial tests indicated the tumor was an Oncocytoma that is a non-cancerous growth. He explained that those tumors were not at all as common in the kidneys as was cancer, never grew to the size of mine, and didn't bleed as mine had. Basically, he didn't trust those initial tests and had ordered additional testing. He explained that 97% of the tumors presenting the characteristics of the one he had removed from me were found to be cancerous.

I completed the telephone conversation with him, maintaining my dignity and calm reserve. I then hung up the phone and shouted for joy. It was as though Isaiah had returned to tell me that God had heard me and had granted me another fifteen years. Doctor Carney had told me not to get my hopes up, but of course, that's just what I did. I couldn't help but be hopeful. It was not that those tests were inconclusive; they clearly indicated that the tumor was benign. Faith, even the size of a mustard seed, would suffice here. Prior to that, I had been assured that the tumor was obvious cancer. I had shifted my prayers from deliverance from cancer to petitions for control of a slow-acting type of Renal Cell Carcinoma and eventual deliverance from the same. Now they were telling me the pathology indicated it was not cancer, "but don't get your hopes up." From that point on, I would have been shocked and confused had the final results of my pathology come back any different than they were. Five days later, the doctor called to certify and confirm that I was among 2% to 3% of folks with kidney tumors like mine that are non-cancerous. By that time, I was not surprised. They had tested and re-tested the tissue and the conclusive results indicated Oncocytoma, not cancer.

Praise and God's Grace

I had cancer; just not kidney cancer. My subsequent treatment for colon cancer was in no way related to the benign Oncocytoma that cost me my right kidney. That colon cancer was small and remained undetected during my kidney surgery and ensuing recovery. The imminent threat of massive Renal Cell Carcinoma had been revoked by the final post-surgical pathology. It was benign. I was elated!

That unexpected clean bill-of-health did present one very significant question. Several persons of faith have inquired as to whether this healing was a matter of God's miraculous intervention to convert a cancerous tumor into a benign tumor or was the tumor always benign but just misdiagnosed with God's healing achieved through more conventional surgery? I assure you that I don't want to detract from God's glory here, but I don't know the answer to that question, and I doubt that any one else knows with any certainty. In either case, to God goes the glory. In either case, it was God's abundant grace I received. I have found that there is a vast difference between knowing what God has done and knowing how God did it. Then, too, God doesn't need my guess-work to enhance his power. Others don't need my guesswork to enhance their faith. Do you suppose John Spong's difficulty in accepting Christ's miraculous healings power has to do with a need to know how God does what He does rather than what He does?

On one hand, the kidney tumor was, both before and

after surgery, diagnosed on the basis of the historical high malignancy rate of kidney tumors. My doctors told me that more than 90% of all tumors found in the kidneys are cancer, regardless of size. This general factor was then combined with the extreme characteristics of size, shape, bleeding tendency, and other cancer-like characteristics particular to my individual tumor. My tumor was very large, had 'pushing-borders,' and was bleeding. Pre-operative needle-biopsies are seldom performed upon renal tumors of this size because they are difficult for the patient, they are somewhat unreliable, and even a benign tumor of this nature would still call for a radical nephrectomy. I don't consider the doctors' diagnosis to have been a misdiagnosis in this case as it reflected the best information available. I believe any other diagnosis would have been reckless.

But then in the midst of this diagnosis came an unbelievable barrage of prayers, spiritual intervention, and very strong faith. First came the word that it was cancer, and then folks prayed, and then came the word that it was not cancer. The sequence was simple: fear and suffering, followed by faith and prayer, followed by deliverance. God intervened to heal me; is it really as important as to just how he did that? One might reason that, had God wanted a truly spectacular healing, God would have made the tumor simply vanish prior to surgery negating the need for surgery. I could argue that the most incredible healing of all would have been for God to intervene to make the tumor disappear prior to the CT Scan. But then no one including myself would have known of the miracle, and then the matter of witness and exposure arises for our consideration.

I suppose we believers do look for miracles so we can champion our own theology to say, "See, I told you so!" Those spectacular healing stories strengthen our faith, and we hope they will strengthen the faith of others. We can certainly find instances in the gospels when Jesus performed just these types of public healings for the very purpose of demonstrating God's power. However, we can also find healings after which Christ cautioned, "Tell no one of this." During my lifetime, I've had any number of medical tests and examinations which resulted in clean bills of health. I wonder; were any of those good test results really unrecognized miraculous healings? Would I be wrong to consider them all healings? I certainly petitioned God for healing prior to each test scheduled because of some symptom or complaint. Would not the most spectacular healing be a person living an illness and injury-free healthy life into his late nineties and then dying a peaceful, pain-free death? Divine physical healing certainly may take on many different forms.

While wandering in the wilderness, the Israelites were bitten by poisonous snakes and many died and others were dying. God told Moses to craft the bronze image of a snake, place it on a pole, and lift it up for all to see. He did just that, and when the snake-bite victims looked up at the bronze snake, they were miraculously healed. Centuries later during the reign of Hezekiah, that bronze statue was still in existence, but by then the image was being worshipped as a god in and of itself. It was my hero King Hezekiah who ordered it destroyed.

I think today we can still focus our attention with such intensity upon the miracle that we are tempted to direct our worship to that miracle and/or the trappings of that miracle, rather than the living God that empowers the miracle. In so doing, we often face great temptation to prioritize and even worship and idolize physical healing as an entity unto itself apart from a proper spiritual relationship with God. Likewise, the healing minister can be idolized and worshipped over and above God's power. It strikes me as a bit odd that some of our current faith-healing personalities claim to maintain a better batting average than did Christ himself. Many infer that there will always be miraculous biological healing if a person has enough faith and mails in enough "seed money." Of course, in real life, we all know that regardless of our faith, we will all in due time encounter a fatal injury or else we will become so sick that we do ultimately die. Sooner or later, biological death becomes a part of this life regardless of the work of faith-healers. We are all dying.

I've long questioned if a denial of or a reluctance to accept the inevitability of eventual death isn't really behind the popularity of such faddish false prophecies as Y2K or date settings for "rapture" when good people are to be simply carried up into the heavens without their physical bodies being subjected to death. As a child, I can remember ministers in their fifties and sixties heralding Nikita Khrushchev as "the anti-Christ." This was supposed to be a sure and certain sign that the rapture was going to happen just any day. At age ten, it all scared me but certainly offered those older ministers an easy way out of their human predicament. Now I'm surprised that my spell-check even recognizes Khrushchev as I realize how false that prophecy was and how convenient that theology was for those who proclaimed it as the gospel truth fifty years ago. Where was their faith and trust? They thought they could avoid death. Even in proclaiming eternal life, Christ acknowledged the predictability of biological death, "*I am the resurrection and the life. Those who believe in me, even though they die, will live, and everyone who lives and believes in me will never die.*"[64]

Judging from current literature, no legitimate writing or reflection about healing and death or near-death or even fear of death is complete without attempting to answer the ultimate death question of theodicy, "Why does an all-powerful, all-loving God allow bad things to happen to good people?" Long ago, Hezekiah struggled with this very question as he suffered. "*Hezekiah turned his face to the wall and prayed to the Lord, Remember O Lord how I have walked before you faithfully and with wholehearted devotion and have done what is good in your eyes." And Hezekiah wept bitterly."* But then my newly found Old Testament hero abruptly changed his tune.

Once he was divinely delivered from his death sentence, Hezekiah quickly abandoned his question of the fairness of God in allowing it to happen to him and moved on to praise God for allowing or even causing near death to transpire in his life in the first place. *"O Lord, your discipline is good and leads to life and health. Oh, heal me and make me live! Yes, now I can see it all – it was good for me to undergo this bitterness, for you have lovingly delivered me from death; you have forgiven all my sins."*[65] I now identify with or relate to Hezekiah's joy and praise, but even in the midst of glorifying God, I must honestly attempt to sort out the reality that not everyone with faith and prayer receives the specific healing they seek. In fact, some die untimely deaths regardless of strong personal faith. Such an acknowledgement does not offend God or even detract from God's Glory; nor should it hamper our faith in God's healing power. Those who cry 'unfair' must pause to consider the all inclusive reach of death. Again, even Lazarus returned to the grave.

"Why does an all-powerful, all-loving God allow bad things to happen to good people?" This is not a new question. It has been asked from patriarchal or even prepatriarchal times with the writing or telling of the story of Job. The book of Job is about persistent faith in the midst of innocent suffering. I believe the story of Job is first and fore-most a love story. *"For God proves his love for us in that while we still were sinners Christ died for us."*[66] I understand the Book of Job is an early Old Testament writing, but it seems to be about God's freely given unconditional love for Job and Job's freely given unconditional love for God in return. True love is a two-way street with neither party placing legalistic conditions upon the other.

In this story, Satan contends that Job loves God solely

because for him to do so insures Job a trouble-free existence. *"Have you not put a fence around him and his house and all that he has, on every side?"*[67] God wants us to freely choose to love Him in return without hope of reward or fear of punishment. In a very practical sense, free will and choice would dissolve if only the unrighteous suffered. There is no such thing as forced love; love absent free will is not love. As John maintains, *"God is Love."*

While our love for God is not motivated by reward, we do know that ultimately all things work together for good for those who love God. Thus, I believe death can very legitimately be called the ultimate healing for the suffering believer. This is especially true if paradise is all Christ claimed it to be. However, I can't help but ponder how someone dying in the midst of Stage Four Renal Cell Carcinoma would react to my story of deliverance from a certain cancer diagnosis. Would either of us dare think, "There but for the grace of God go I?" In reality, the grace of God is the one thing we both receive and share in sufficient portion. It is the common denominator.

The dying person may be delivered from death, but eventually we will all be delivered by death. I think it takes far more faith to pray, "Thy will be done" than it takes to pray, "Heal me, Lord." Through God's grace and love and God-given faith we can all rejoice in the miraculous healing of another. Our faith can be strengthened and our hope renewed. *"Yes, this anguish was good for me, for you have rescued me from death; and forgiven all my sins."*[68] As with Hezekiah, I have learned to accept death by being delivered from death. I have learned to embrace suffering as a blessed direct link to a suffering/loving God. I have learned to wait for God.

God healed me. I don't know just how God accomplished that task, but I thanked God and I continue to thank God. The "power of positive thinking" has now become a mere by-product of God's holy presence. I am a far better priest for having this experience, and I now have a spiritual point of personal reference. That familiar, deep, abiding spiritual awareness of eternal life remains with me and serves as a constant reminder that God will be with me when I eventually need him most.

Peter Gomes preaches about miracles and declares, *"The question to be put about a miracle is not 'Is it true?' Or even 'How can this be?' but rather 'What does this say?' At its essence a miracle is a message – an illustration or a demonstration of a message that God chooses to communicate to us. A miracle is God's extraordinary message in the midst of the ordinary,....."*[69] I really like this explanation and know it to be true in my case. God's message for me can be summed up as, "Wait for me, don't fear for I am with you even in the midst of suffering."

Of course, there is a far greater value derived from this miracle, this message and this time of fear and suffering than merely my personal preparation for death. The experience was life-changing for both Judy and me, and we have since had many long discussions about this unexpected episode and its impact upon our lives together. We are both duly impressed and now both of us recognize it all as a real wake-up call from God. We are taking this time to readjust our attitudes and priorities. We are seeking God's will for what we thought we had previously resolved. We are still listening to that extraordinary message from God. We are seeking God's will for our marriage, our relationships with our children and our ministries. We are learning to pray more sincerely "Thy will be done," and then to carefully consider the possible implications of such a trusting prayer. It may not have seemed like it when we were younger, but we've always faced an uncertain future. Our plans for the future have become less specific and more adaptable. Material possessions now seem so inconsequential. Now we seem to better understand the wisdom of Christ's advice, "Seek ye first the Kingdom of God."

In reflection, I have attempted to summarize the

understandings we have gained or better realized through that summer's Hezekiah experience. In so doing, I begin to appreciate just what all we've been through and all of the many and varied lessons we learned in such a very short period of time. My inventory of lessons learned seems so inadequate and abbreviated. Of course, some of these lessons remain deeply spiritual and dwell far beyond my ability to put into words. Others are of a more practical and tangible nature and herein warrant some clarification and synopsis. However, struggling to keep in mind Merton's caveat, *"Suffer without imposing on others a theory of suffering…,"* I list the following brief inventory not as guidance for others, rather as an outline from my own personal spiritual reflection. Should someone find some form or extent of personal relevance in these musings then so be it, but such is not my primary intention.

Now that chaotic summer is behind me, and I reflect upon the following:

~   God is Love
~   God Suffers
~   Death Belongs to This Life
~   <u>Faith</u> is the Best Preparation for Death
~   <u>Waiting</u> for God is a Crucial Part of that Faith
~   <u>Doing</u> the Gospel is a Crucial Part of that Waiting
~   Some will be Miraculously but Temporarily Delivered from Death
~   All Believers will eventually be delivered from Death By Death
~   We are not alone / we will never be alone

Believing, waiting, and doing are the action verbs of dying. This formula includes love, community, and suffering. "Faith in God," "waiting for God," and "doing the Gospel" really are my best remedies for death this side of death. I trust God is my best remedy for death on that other unknown side of death. As for my eventual biological death itself, I can only turn to the suffering Christ upon the cross. I don't know where else to turn. This seems like such a "no-brainer" for me. Again, for me, any other option would only lead to total despair and abandonment, ultimately leading to the absolute and final cessation of all life. I place all my hope for life upon that two thousand year old Roman execution. I understand it a little better having suffered. Jesus promised that all those who believed in him would not perish. Scholars can play all the linguistic and contextual games they want with that English word "perish," but its common connotation will stand. I can't fathom non-existence; I believe Christ. All of these years later and no one has come along with a better promise.

I know the cross represents suffering, but even that seems like an attractive option to non-existence. This is especially the case when I realize that I'm not the Messiah; I don't have to be crucified. He absorbed that sting of death for me. But he did tell me to pick up my own cross and follow him, and I can do that. It's not that I am afraid of non-existence; it is simply that I reject it. God created me with a mind that cannot process the concept of my own non-existence. Thus I refuse to perish. God equipped me with a mind that knows and understands eternity. By God, I choose life! With Christ, no power in this world is going to hold me down! I know these are very big words from a little man, but they come from a little man who has a very big God indeed!

Again, this is my experience, my thinking, my faith, and my attitude. I wouldn't force this approach upon any other person if I could or even wanted to. Some others will choose to follow a different path. I deeply respect them, love them, and honor their dignity and that God given right to choose. But I also exercised that same right for myself as the summer days grew shorter and faded into autumn, and I blindly and rather abruptly faced another valley in the shadows; a second diagnosis of cancer.

Where is the Glory?

My second diagnosis of cancer led to additional bible study and reflection which, in turn, led to a new bible character of focus. Ichabod is, of course, a Bible name and a Bible character. The name was not all that exceptional for men in their sixties and seventies when I was a child. Therefore, I've always stereotyped the name considering it an "old man's name." So, I am somewhat surprised to find we only know the biblical Ichabod as a new-born babe. But Ichabod's birth brought none of the happy excitement, joy, and hope commonly associated with the arrival of a new baby. This baby was born in the midst of despair, disillusionment, tragedy, and a questioned future. Ichabod's very name presents a forlorn and cynical question.

Ichabod was born about a thousand years before Christ to a scoundrel of a priest by the name of Phinehas and his unfortunate wife. His grandfather was the good priest Eli who was overweight, blind, and in his late nineties by the time Ichabod came into the world. His mother was near her time of delivery when her husband Phinehas marched off to an ill-conceived war against the Philistines. He marched with the Israelite army and helped carry the Ark of the Covenant of God at the head of the army column as sort of a talisman for added safety and protection. This shallow and self-serving manipulation of God's very presence downright troubled Eli and, in time, his worries proved justified as the Philistines overwhelmed and defeated the Israelite army, killed both

Phinehas and his brother Hophni, and of most importance, captured the sacred Ark of the Covenant.

When a runner brought Eli the shocking news of the capture of the Ark and the death of his two sons, it all proved more shocking and stressful than the old priest could manage. Upon receiving the news, he fell out of his chair, broke his neck, and died on the spot. Thus, that terrible news was compounded by Eli's death and then carried to Phinehas' wife, who went into immediate labor, gave birth to a boy, and then died from the childbirth. Prior to her death, she named her newborn son Ichabod which means, "Where is the glory?"

The ark was gone; the glory had left Jerusalem. Where was it? Well, for a very brief time, it was with the Philistines! But as you can imagine, the Philistines soon realized the Ark of the Covenant, which was inhabited by the presence of the living God, did not make for the best war trophy. They first carried it into the temple of their God "Dagon" in the Philistine town of Ashdod, and of much interest, Ashdod and its surrounding villages were struck by a plague of tumors. Many people were dying and suffering from the tumors so they moved it to the town of Gath and those townspeople were also struck with similar tumors. Thus, they attempted to move it to Ekron, but those folks saw it coming from a distance and mounted a vigorous public protest. As the tumors spread across their community, the frantic people petitioned their national leaders to return the Ark to the Israelites. It was indeed a holy hot potato.

The Philistine leaders called for their spiritual diviners who, in the interest of halting the plague of tumors, advised them to return the Ark to Israel. In so doing, these diviners were perhaps initiating the world's first recorded cancer awareness and prevention program. I don't want to draw too much of a parallel here, other than to note that these ancient and pagan diviners were motivated to prevent further death and suffering caused by tumors. They also suggested that the leaders include a guilt offering of gold, five pieces of which were to be sculpted or molded into the shape of tumors. The leaders accepted the advice and had the gold along with those five little precious metal tumors and the Ark itself carted back to Israel. In time, the Ark was carried back to the remote Israeli town of Kiriath-Jearim where it remained for twenty years until David could be crowned King and lead an army to escort the Ark of the Covenant all the way back to Jerusalem where it really belonged.

An ark is a box or container, and a covenant is a contract or agreement between two parties based upon trust, faith, and love. Moses, on behalf of God's people and God, entered into a covenant at Sinai. God promised, *"You shall worship the Lord your God, and I will bless your bread and water; and I will take sickness away from you."*[70] The covenant called for the people to worship, obey, and love God and for God to protect, be present among, and love the people. That was the Covenant. God summoned Moses to the top of the mountain and sealed this holy pact with tablets of stone bearing the Ten Commandments which recorded that Covenant and served as a basic set of instruction for implementing and maintaining the agreement.

To the modern-day Trinitarian Christian, those stone tablets encompass the first part of a three-part divine writing. In Holy Scripture, we find that God the Parent wrote in cold stone, God the Son of Man wrote in the dirt, and according to St. Paul, God the Holy Spirit writes upon our hearts. All three of these writings reflect the very presence of the living God. For God's people of the great exodus, those stone tablets represented God's presence, and they were to be kept in the Holy of Holies, a place where God chose to reveal himself from time to time to the select representatives of those chosen people.

God gave the tablets to Moses along with specifications for a container or an ark in which that covenant could be kept.

"Have the people make an Ark of acacia wood – a sacred chest 45 inches long, 27 inches wide and 27 inches high. Overlay it inside and outside with pure gold, and run a molding of gold all around it. Cast four gold rings and attach them to its four feet, two rings on each side. Make poles from acacia wood, and overlay them with gold. Insert the poles into the rings at the sides of the Ark to carry it."[71] Upon completion, the tablets bearing the Ten Commandments were placed inside the Ark, thus comprising the Ark of the Covenant or what King David came to refer to as God's footstool.

This was the Ark Phinehas and Hophni were foolish enough to fatally carry into battle and then lost into the hands of the victorious Philistines. This footstool was the war prize the Philistines were so quick and willing to relinquish following the plagues of tumors and resulting widespread deaths. This was the presence of the living God that was eventually carried to a house on a hill in that small and remote town of Kiriath-Jearim in Israel. The tumors and the deaths did not follow the Ark to Kiriath-Jearim. Had Ichabod's broken-hearted mother lived another seven months, she could have found a positive answer to her cynical question. The Glory had returned to Israel. The presence of God was out there among God's own people.

I was initially attracted to the story of Ichabod and the Ark upon learning of my second diagnosis of cancer following so closely upon the heels of my first victorious healing. Just as Hezekiah's early tears and fears seemed to parallel my own, so too the despair, disillusionment, and loss of glory surrounding Ichabod's birth seemed very relevant to my second diagnosis and resulting despair. I, too, was asking the Ichabod question, "Where has the glory gone?" While it was not to be found with Ichabod, he did lead me to a humble priest named Eleazar of Kiriath-Jearim.

In reading of that grand and glorious day in that remote Israeli town, I stumbled upon a quiet man named Eleazar who now serves as my Bible hero for my second season in the valley of the shadow of cancer. More like me and less like the flamboyant King Hezekiah, Eleazar was not a man of great prominence. This Eleazar was the humble son of Amminadab and not to be confused with about six other biblical Eleazars including sons of Aaron, Dodo (whoever that was), Mahli, Phinehas (not related to Ichabod's dad), and Eliud. Nor is my hero to be confused with the eleven biblical Eliezers whose name presents a slightly different spelling and therefore a slightly different meaning. My Eleazar's name means "God is helper," and I would certainly need God as my helper. I needed God to help me get through this second valley of shadows.

The Ark was carried to Eleazar's father's house there on top of a hill in Kiriath-Jearim where it remained for twenty years. Eleazar was ordained to care for and safe-guard the Ark for the years it was to remain at Amminadab's house. Eleazar served as a caretaker for that holy covenant between humankind and God during a very intense and difficult time in the life of that divine relationship. All was not well in Israel as the absence of the Ark from its rightful place in Jerusalem reflected the turbulent times of King Saul and the rise of his successor, King David. Still, the Ark came safely back into Israel with "God as helper," a faithful Eleazar, functioning to answer the question posed by Ichabod's dying mother, "Where is the Glory?" With God's help, Eleazar could proclaim to all that no matter the strife amid apparent endless difficulties, the presence of the living God is still among His chosen people. God's glory is with us throughout the ups and downs of our battle with cancer.

That second diagnosis seemed to bring a brief and temporary but awful loss of the presence of God. It seemed as though I had lost God's glory, God's holiness, and His peace. The Letter to the Hebrews advises us to *"Pursue peace with everyone, and the holiness without which no one can see the Lord."*[72] In the face of cancer, we crave peace. But what about the second part of that sentence that counsels us to pursue holiness. In our suffering, dare we actually chase after holiness?

Years ago, while still the Chief of Police in Council Bluffs, Iowa, I first felt called to jail ministry. I could hardly minister in my own jail, so I started ministering in the Omaha jail just across the Missouri River. One Sunday afternoon, I was walking down a long hallway in that jail, carrying my Bible and prayer book on the way to conduct one of my first worship services. A trustee was working there alone, mopping the floor, and as I passed by, he asked me if I was a priest. I answered, "No - I'm a volunteer assistant chaplain." He responded, "Oh, I knew you were some sort of Holy Man." His comment scared me, and then my awkward response confused both him and me. I quickly replied, "Oh, I'm no Holy Man" and continued on my way to chapel. In more than twenty years of police work, I had been called a lot of things, but never before had anyone ever called me Holy, and that adjective just didn't seem to fit. It made me feel uneasy and even hypocritical.

I suspect many of us are a bit uneasy with this concept of personal holiness, but that Hebrews reading tells us to "pursue holiness." We know God is Holy, but are we really a Holy people? If we are so holy, why must we continually be confessing our sins, all those things we've done wrong and all those good things we've left undone?

On our own, under our own spiritual power, if we are honest with ourselves, we know we are not holy. But the author of the Book of Hebrews tells us to at least run the race in pursuit of holiness. And I suspect we often run both in pursuit of it and at the same time, in fear of it. We can sincerely go through the motions. We may be willing to pursue holiness, but we don't necessarily ever want to catch up with it. Peter and James and John caught up with Holiness on the mount of transfiguration, and they were terrified.

We remember Isaiah's familiar and very honest exclamation when he caught up with holiness; "*Woe is me! Woe is me, I am lost, for I am a man of unclean lips, and I live among a people of unclean lips.*" We remember Christ's perfection and quite naturally we say woe is me. We remember Isaiah's unclean lips, but we forget the seraph with a live burning coal taken from the altar; we forget that grand and glorious angel who proclaimed, "Now that this has touched your lips, your guilt has departed and your sin is blotted out."

Your holiness may sound a bit awkward, but through His grace, you are a Holy Man. You are a Holy Woman. That trustee in the Omaha Jail all those years ago was right; I am a holy-man. We are a holy people simply because of God's grace. Our disease and suffering doesn't make us holy, but perhaps it can motivate us to pursue holiness. We are called by God to chase after Holiness, but we dare not run such a race in competition with one another, less we develop a holier than thou attitude. Competition may be a healthy thing in many aspects of life, but never in Christian spirituality. In fact, it can be the cause of much division and strife. We dare not run this holy race with arrogance or a feeling of self-sufficiency for such is the stuff hypocrisy is made of. Likewise, we dare not give up the race because of loss and despair brought on by illness. Phinehas and Hophni should have never carried the holiness of the Ark of the Covenant into battle against the Philistines. However, the holiness of the cross is well suited for the battle against cancer.

Heart Washing

Directional signs and arrows dominated the overhead space of the long hospital corridor. I walked along at a fairly brisk pace as I searched for a familiar sign, and then realized I was no longer looking for "urology." That was all behind me now. My three-month post-surgical CT Scan was clean, and my urologist Dr. Carney had given me the "all clear" sign. I was healed. However, it was now time for my three-year routine colonoscopy, and early that morning, I was searching for a sign that read G I (or gastro-intestinal) Lab.

I had been in that same examination center for the same test with the same doctor just three years earlier. Three years earlier my good friend Dan was fighting for his life in a struggle with colon cancer, and that had prompted me to undergo my first colonoscopy. I can remember how terrified I was prior to that first colon examination and how amazed I was that it had proved to be so painless and unproblematic. I had listened to a lot of old stories about fearsome old techniques and equipment that had long since been discontinued. During that first procedure, my doctor found and removed three small benign polyps as I relaxed and watched on a table-side television set. There was no pain or great discomfort. The Doc told me to return for my next follow-up exam in three years, and I was there early for that purpose and truly expected only to encounter similar small polyps in a worse-case scenario.

The doctor finished the exam and then came to talk to

me as I waited for the sedation to wear off. He told me he had found a mass about two centimeters in diameter, and he could not remove it. He explained there were characteristics with its appearance that concerned him. I responded, "You mean it could be cancer?" He replied yes and said he had taken a biopsy and would let me know the results. The following afternoon he called to tell me that the biopsy indicated that it was cancer. He gave me the name and telephone number of a good colon-rectal surgeon and told me to call for an appointment.

The next day, I called the recommended surgeon's office, explained my cancer diagnosis and referral, and asked the scheduler for an appointment. She explained that the soonest the doctor could see me was twenty-three days later. I had been down this uncertain and unknowing road before. This time, however, the doctor who performed the test had at least expressed a guarded expectation that the tumor had been caught early enough to avoid catastrophic consequences. Still, I now knew there was a cancer growing in my bowls, and I dreaded that lengthy wait just for an initial meeting with a prospective surgeon.

I still had Jeff's cell phone number plugged into my speed dial, so I gave him a call. He was very prompt to return my call and expressed genuine concern and compassion. Without hesitation, he promised he would set me up with the best oncological surgeon at Emory's Winship Cancer Institute. He soon called me back and explained that the surgeon would see me the following week. I thanked Dr. Carney and got off the phone so he could return to his busy schedule. I then offered yet another prayer of thanksgiving for God providing me with such a fine physician.

The following week, I walked into the oncological surgery department at the Winship Cancer Institute. I noticed a large sign near the entry that cited the Hebrew Proverb 17:22, "*A cheerful heart is good medicine.*" With some irony and cynicism, it occurred to me that this isolated proverb so strategically placed was really little more than a clever bit of "brainwashing." I was entering there to be told that they were going to cut me open with a knife for the second time in four months, and I was supposed to be happy. The thought of brainwashing lingered just long enough for me to realize the Proverb actually made no mention of the brain; rather it spoke of the heart. This was not brainwashing. The heart reflects a concept of spirituality rather than intellect, and I began to toy with the self-invented turn of the phrase, "heartwashing."

As I sat in the waiting room pondering my new-found catch phrase, I began to notice pale, thin people with wigs, hats, and bandanas covering their balding heads. I was immediately ashamed of my self-pity and cynicism and noticed that there was a calm cheerfulness among these folks. There was no jolly laughter, but there were some sweet smiles, and I found those smiles contagious. This was indeed "heartwashing," but it had little to do with any sign on the wall. It was a real emotional cleansing and emanated from the hearts of my fellow cancer sufferers. This was real love of neighbor and reminded me of the spiritual wisdom of Ecclesiastes which reads, "*Sorrow is better than laughter, for by sadness of countenance the heart is made glad.*"[73] There is far more to true joy than hilarity and merriment. Laughter is common, but there is a far deeper peace, hope, and comfort that reveal a true spiritual joy which in turn makes for very good medicine for the mind and the body. I don't believe such can be contrived or manipulated as I suspect that in the midst of suffering, such joy is derived from God's love.

My reflections were pleasantly interrupted by the arrival of my niece Amanda who is a Registered Nurse and was there to encourage me and add a little medical knowledge to the questions I might ask of the doctor, or I should say doctors. I encountered no assembly line approach at Winship.

No one seemed to be in a big hurry as I was made to feel like my illness was significant and warranted serious attention. When my surgeon entered the examining room, he was accompanied by three other doctors. I am aware that this was such primarily because Emory is both a medical school and a research hospital. However, it remains quite reassuring to receive that degree and intensity of care.

The doctor who would be doing the surgery had viewed the films of the tumor and the report of the biopsy taken during the colonoscopy. He explained that my tumor was not exceptionally large and was located high in the upper transcending section of the colon. He assured me the need for a colostomy was highly unlikely and explained that he wanted to do a simple resection of the colon to remove the tumor, surrounding lymph tissue and blood supply. He said that radiation would not be an option and pre-surgical chemotherapy was not required. He offered me a surgery date for this necessary procedure that was only two weeks hence, and I accepted, knowing that I would be having the surgery at the same time I was scheduled for my initial visit with the previously referred surgeon.

My surgeon provided much additional information as Amanda took notes. Again, there were no ironclad guarantees, but most of what he said was encouraging. This was indeed different from my first diagnosis. Here was hope. I left with my spirits lifted, knowing that there was hope, and that once again, I did not face a lengthy and tense period of waiting for surgery. I walked out past the Hebrew Proverb sign on the wall with a cheerful heart knowing that I was indeed blessed by God. My heart had been washed by the good cheer of the other patients who were simply going about the business of living. My heart had been washed by the encouragement of a good doctor who was simply going about the business of healing.

I have been in and out of the cancer center on numerous

occasions since, and I remain deeply impressed with a spirit of love, joy, and healing that so abounds there. I witnessed one brief negative flare-up that was converted almost immediately to a humorous and even healing episode thanks to the love of a good wife. I was seated in the crowded blood-lab waiting room awaiting my turn for samples to be drawn when a nurse or tech escorted an elderly couple in and seated them. She explained, "Just wait here, and they will call your name."

Not more than five minutes passed before the same nurse reappeared and said, "I'm sorry, I've brought you to the wrong lab. We need to move down the hall to another waiting room."

At that moment, the old man jumped to his feet with surprising energy and burst into a very inappropriate diatribe. His inappropriate words seemed especially harsh and caustic because of the presence of so many who were patiently suffering so much. He shouted at the nurse, "Why did you bring us here if this is not where we're supposed to be? Don't you know your job? Our time is valuable! We have better things to do than sit here all day while you get your act together."

He inhaled to get the air needed to continue his harangue, when his small wife sat erect and in a less loud but far more commanding voice simply said, "Oh, shut up!" Those words echoed throughout the now silent waiting room. To the husband's redeeming credit, he did just that and uttered not another sound. The wife turned to the nurse and said, "It is ok, honey, if you just point us in the right direction, we will find it." Of course, the nurse escorted them out of the waiting room and down the hall to the correct lab. Those who remained exchanged smiling glances.

The episode had been comic but very evocative for me. It reminded me of how important it was to have a strong spouse in times of life's crisis. I really don't think I could have made it through my shadowed valleys without Judy. Judy is and has always been a strong woman who loves me very much but knows how to think for herself and take decisive action on her own when necessary. I remember in the 70's and 80's when it was popular in the more conservative wing of the church to focus upon the role of the wife in the home. Women's Bible studies were notorious for instilling in woman the proper balance of her biblically mandated submissiveness to the husband who was to be the head of the house. Curriculum developers apparently cherry-picked some of St. Paul's more culture-based writings to the disregard of Christ's revolutionary approach to women.

Judy attended some of those Bible studies and recognized that the submissive approach would not work with a husband who wanted an equal partner rather than a high-maintenance subordinate helper. We each have our strengths and weaknesses and take the lead in matters that best reciprocate those strengths. It has worked for more than four decades now. Now I wonder how couples manage life's crises when only one has taken the lead in all matters. If that head of the house is incapacitated and unable to physically lead, how does the submissive one take charge? It must be very difficult. As I lay in intensive care, it was reassuring for me to know that Judy was taking care of our home and family.

Instant Replay

It had been almost three months since I had received word that my kidney tumor was totally benign, and needless to say, I had been reveling in the joy and God's glory of it all. Only one woman in my congregation had the foresight to caution me to be careful with "mountain-top" experiences, and her words of warning echoed back to help me rationalize this completely new and unexpected discouraging turn of events. Why would God let this happen to me? Why would God heal me of a large tumor on a kidney only to have me suffer colon cancer? Where was the glory in that?

In the 8th Chapter of Mark's Gospel, Christ told his disciples that he had to undergo great suffering. God forbid it, Lord! I'll not have a God who suffers, for that kind of God might expect me to suffer also. You think? *"If any want to become my followers, let them deny themselves and take up their cross."*[74] He was not talking about the gold pendant bought at Zale's. He was talking about suffering. The cross is an instrument of pain, even the cross we ourselves are to take up.

I believe it takes a committed faith to pray, "Thy will be done." Of course, none of this precludes the fact that it is God's will to heal us. As made clear earlier, I believe in God's healing power. We ought to pray with faith asking for healing. But Jesus prayed, "Father, if you are willing, remove this cup from me; yet not my will but yours be done!" Don't put your faith in healing, put it in God. Trust that His will is best for you. Christ didn't say take up your Easter morn empty tomb and follow me, He said take up your cross.

Our suffering and willingness to suffer, to take up our cross, has much to do with "who" we say Christ is. The letter to the Hebrews discusses pain and suffering. The author of that letter writes about Jesus, "*It is fitting that God should make the founder of our salvation, perfect through suffering. Because he himself was tested by what he suffered, he is able to help those of us who suffer.*"[75]

Jesus was badly beaten, tortured, and then nailed to a cross. He was thirsty and asked for something to drink. Mark tells us the soldiers brought him a cup of wine mixed with gall, and this was, of course, very bitter to the taste. Some interpret this as a further mocking of Christ. However, most recognize wine mingled with an opiate as a common first century painkiller. It was a drug that was specifically used back in those times to ease the pain of dying. In fact, the soldiers were most likely offering some compassion, rather than further mockery. Jesus tasted the concoction, recognized what it was, and he rejected it. With all apologies to Martin Scorsese, that was the last temptation of Christ.

In fairness, Scorsese is an entertainer, not a theologian. One probably ought not to go to church for entertainment or to Hollywood for theology. Some found value in the controversial film, "The Last Temptation of Christ." But I didn't like it primarily because of Christ's question, "Who do you say that I am?" Who the movie says Jesus was, and who I say he is, are wholly incompatible concepts. The movie presents a Jesus who calls "fear" his "god," and he talks about being motivated more by fear than by love.

The detractors of the faith would much prefer a God who is fear. A "Fear God" can be easily denigrated. However, the world can't cope with a suffering God. A God, who is both strong enough, and at the same time vulnerable enough to suffer and die, is just too stark, too intense, and too formidable for them to so casually shelve. Have you noticed that for more than two thousand years now the world has been unable to simply ignore someone they purportedly don't even believe in? Does that tell us something? A suffering God is a fearsome God, and at the same time, he is a loving God. Such a God cannot be casually dismissed just as our faith in Him in the midst of our suffering cannot be dismissed.

He would not drink of that cup; and we wonder why not? It might have made unbearable pain bearable. He refused to drink because he was the Messiah for all, even for those who die young and violently and without the benefit of pain-killing narcotics. It was necessary for him to suffer. He came to earth to know and to experience life as it really is, and we know life can be very painful at times. Take up your cross and follow Him. Where was the glory in my second diagnosis? There is glory in the cross.

The prophet Amos once prophesied of a man who struggled to free himself from a lion only to run into a bear. Twenty seven hundred years later, I felt like that man. I struggled with that lion called Renal Cell Carcinoma, and with God's help I broke free. That lion got one of my kidneys and left a big scar, but I had a kidney to spare, and I had made good my escape. Then, just as I was running free from the lion, a big old ugly bear called Colon Cancer came out of the woods and grabbed me. Like Ichabod's mother, my first reaction was to ask, "Where is the glory?"

I had declared that God's message for me in that first healing could be summarized as, "Wait for me and don't fear. I am with you even in the midst of suffering." I was patiently waiting for God, and I was no longer afraid, but somehow I got the idea that my suffering was over and done with for good. That was more of a naive assumption than spiritual or even intellectual reflection. I forgot I still had a cross to carry. How can one be so miraculously delivered and yet still suffer? How can one be so elated one moment, and so perplexed the next? Why did I have to return to the pain?

Luke's Gospel brings us the short story of the ten lepers that Jesus healed, with only one of them, one lowly Samaritan, taking the time and the common courtesy to return to Christ to say "Thank you!" I think my parents favorite question for me when I was a child had to be, "Did you tell the man thank you?" "Did you say thank you to the nice lady?" Eventually, I came to understand it was the right thing to do.

That Luke scripture passage makes for a great Sunday school lesson for children learning good manners, but I think there is far more involved in Christ's follow-up encounter with the one leper than merely that basic lesson of common courtesy. Luke didn't include this story in his Gospel just to tell us that Jesus wants us to be polite. At least, that is not the core teaching of this brief episode.

I don't think the nine lepers failed to return simply because they were rude people. I believe the nine did not return primarily because it would have been very unpleasant for them. To get to Christ, they would have had to go back to that place and among those folks who knew them as lepers, and they had left all of that behind. To go back would have forced them to embrace their ugly past.

In those days, leprosy was commonly thought to be the direct result of, or at least related to, or somehow symbolic, of sin. As wrong as it seems to us today, at the time Luke wrote his Gospel there was great shame in having the disease of leprosy. Lepers were the untouchables of that day, and now those folks were no longer lepers. Now that they were healed, they were free to mingle with the in-crowd, and they were free to look down their noses at those shameful, dirty, rotting, foul-smelling untouchables. They were now clean and righteous; at least, on the outside.

For each of us in our own way, truthfully claiming our own past can be a very difficult struggle indeed. Author L. Gregory Jones writes about loving oneself and forgiving one's self. *"Those struggles require us to take time to learn to identify and name those features of our past that most haunt us."*[76] To be sure, there is no shame in having cancer or being a cancer survivor. With perhaps very rare exception, no one today relates disgrace or indignity to cancer patients.

I found the story of the lepers related to an even deeper meaning for me in my return to a second diagnosis of cancer. I found it relating to my very identity as perceived by others. While I had significantly changed spiritually during my first diagnosis, I was still me. However, for some, I seemed to take on the identity of the disease itself. Sort of like "the ten lepers" rather than the ten persons with leprosy. When I would tell some folks of my initial diagnosis, I sensed that for them I had become the disease. I became cancer that just happened to be Mark, rather than Mark who just happened to have cancer. We do this very commonly with mental illness, developmental disabilities, and other challenges we either don't understand or fear. He is "a schizophrenic" rather than a person suffering schizophrenia. A lame person becomes a "cripple." She is a "Down's baby." No, she is not; she is a baby who experiences Down's syndrome. She is a person. This is far more than merely "politically correct" language. Our words directly reflect our love for God and neighbor. Our neighbors are more than the challenges they encounter. We are more than the challenges we face. We are children of God created in His image with or without cancer.

In part, I dreaded going back to being a cancer patient as I sought to shirk that falsely imposed erroneous identity. Of course, there are other social stigmas wrongfully relegated to cancer sufferers by unthinking and/or uninformed others. Such folks mean well and genuinely want to show compassion, but they and their words can make it so difficult for us to "go back." I felt the single most inappropriate reaction to me in my suffering was excessive sympathy or pity. A little compassion, understanding, and empathy are much welcomed. A visit is truly valued, calls and cards are appreciated, but pity is an unwelcome guest. Pity is a rude guest who demeans the host.

Also, others' fear of the disease adds yet another dimension to their inappropriate reaction to our illness. On occasions, conversations would reveal an attitude of, "Thank God it's not me!" You should be aware that your cancer can strike fear in the hearts of some others. Not fear of contagion, but fear of the odds. Cancer is on the increase, and just one more friend with the diagnosis is not what others want to hear. I imagine it is threatening in a sense of personal encroachment. Perhaps they feel increased vulnerability due to the increased numbers alone.

Luke tells us all ten lepers were healed physically. But only the lone Samaritan who returned was told by Christ, "Get up and go on your way; your faith has made you well." All ten had enough faith to call out to Christ for mercy. They called him master. They had enough faith in him to follow his command to go to the priests. Make no mistake about it; they were all healed of leprosy. But I wonder if they were made truly and completely whole? Was that healing a completed act? Did they receive healing for the pain and memory of their past, or did they live out their days haunted by the memory of that awful past, the false identity, the self doubts, the poor self-esteem, and the fear that someone, someday, somewhere might say, "Wait just a minute; I know you! I remember you from that tiny village near the border of Samaria and Galilee. You used to sit there in the dirt and dust beside the road and beg. You are a leper!"

The Samaritan who returned to Christ was more than just healed; he was made completely well because, as Luke says, "He turned back." He turned back to Christ. Jones also writes, "*We typically can't do this alone. We need each other as we learn how to take the time to narrate our own and one another's stories, how to identify the bearing of our pasts on*

the present, in the context of the practices and friendships
of Christian community."[77] There is indeed mighty healing
power within this Christian Community, the extended body
of Christ on earth. I have found it easier to travel life's more
arduous journeys in the company of believers.

It now appears as though I am becoming better at traveling through these valleys. The Psalmist would make it
seem as though there was only one valley of the shadow of
death. But now I know there are in fact many valleys scat-
tered throughout this rugged mountain range called life.
Hopefully there are not as many shadowy valleys as there
are grand mountain tops, but just the same, we must brace
ourselves for more than one valley in life. As I came down
off the mountain top and entered this second season of my
valley journey, I realized that I was far better prepared and
equipped because of my trek through that first valley.

In some ways, I was traveling a lot lighter. I left behind
much of my fear of the dying process. I still didn't want to
die, but I almost immediately found great peace in the spiritual discernment of the eternal within me. I was prepared
to wait for God, but that proved completely unnecessary in
dealing with my fears. This second time, I knew enough not
to try to go it on my own according to my own expectations
and plans. The second time around, the words, "Thy will
be done" came a lot easier and much sooner. I can honestly
say my faith in God's power to heal was not shaken in the
least. This new diagnosis did not undo the significance of
my miraculous delivery from the first. The cancer was not
spreading. This was a new primary tumor and was in no way
related to the first. That was a lion; this new monster was a
bear. Thank God they lived in different valleys on opposite
sides of that glorious mountain.

But the second diagnosis so took me by surprise that
I became more perplexed than anxious, more baffled than
doubtful. Where was the glory? Oh, how I relished basking

in that glory by telling others of my healing. Now I was in trouble again, and so soon. What was God trying to tell me? What had I done wrong? What was I doing wrong? Just when I finally had it all figured out, I was thrown a curve. Yes, it was a shame that I had to go through a second major abdominal surgery in such quick order, but really, "What was God up to, now?" What was it that was obstructing my understanding? Once again, I was trying to reason my way through a physical crisis, and in doing so, I was at risk of letting it become a spiritual crisis.

Once again, I worried, wrestled with emotions, read, and prayed even as I knew I could only let go and wait for God's timing in this new challenge. I even returned to my summer's writing and found a line from my own words that came crashing in on me to remind me just what God expected from me again that fall. "Faith in Love," and "faith and love" carried me through that summer. Again, my reasoning was no match for God's wisdom and love. I simply needed to have faith in that God who is love. I needed to believe. I needed to take up my cross and follow Him. My prayer had been, 'Thy will be done!' Did I really have enough faith in God's love to truly believe that his will would be best for me? I needed to drink in and draw strength and patience from the love that, with such abundance, surrounded and embraced me.

I knew from the spiritual aftermath of my first diagnosis that the foremost principle of the Christian faith is life over death. I had faced natural death with an understanding and acceptance of eternal spiritual life and how it is absolutely inseparable from faith and love. I had embraced life, faith, and love as the Easter message. I had read John's gospel and found where Christ pronounced, *"I give them eternal life, and they will never perish. No one will snatch them out of my hand. What my Father has given me is greater than all else, and no one can snatch it out of the Father's hand. The Father and I are one."*[78]

The remarkable 68th Psalm was composed somewhere around 700 years before Christ taught of eternal life; yet in its 20th verse, we could find as graphic and natural an Easter message as we will find anywhere in Holy Scripture. *"God is for us a God of deliverance; God the Lord provides an escape from death."*[79] That line grabs us because we all want to escape death, and yet we know we all face a biological death. Let's be honest, we share that fear and that dread. We are all in this thing together. However, because we are created in God's image, we also each carry within our souls the inborn, innate, unquenchable desire to live forever. God is forever, we are in God's image, and so, in that image, we want to live forever and we shall. That is the "Good News." Because of our faith and because of God's love, we will live forever.

The young man was dressed in white and was seated inside the open tomb. The three women entered the tomb, and he said to them, *"You are looking for Jesus of Nazareth who was crucified. He has been raised!"* These same three women were there at the crucifixion and watched precious life-sustaining blood flow from the nail-punctured hands and feet. They watched as it trickled down across the rough hewn wood grain and into the dust at the foot of the cross. Remember that you are dust and to dust you shall return. But now, He has been raised! Because he was truly human, he returned to the dust – because He was truly God, He was raised. We will return to the dust, but because we are baptized into his death, we, too, shall be raised.

Easter is so much more than some quaint little 'alls-well-that-ends-well' story. For those who believe, that is the story of our life and death and eternal life after death. That celebration is about so much more than Spring-time and flowers. That is not a story about chocolate Easter bunnies and pastel colored eggs. It is a story about flesh and blood, about life and death.

Where is the Love?

In my perplexed and confused suffering, I was asking God the Ichabod question of "Where is the Glory?" It seemed to have departed from me, leaving only human suffering. But Kitamori wrote, *"Theology of Glory' can be understood only through 'theology of the cross.' God's love can be understood only on the basis of his pain. His glory is to be understood only on the basis of his pain. His glory is the radiance of the cross; his love is the victory of his pain. Our task then is to comprehend the depth of Christ's love as God's pain."*[80] He then cites Ephesians 3:16–19, *"I pray that, according to the riches of his glory, he may grant that you may be strengthened in your inner being with power through his spirit, and that Christ may dwell in your hearts through faith, as you are being rooted and grounded in love. I pray that you may have the power to comprehend, with all the saints, what is the breadth and length and height and depth, and to know the love of Christ that surpasses knowledge, so that you may be filled with all the fullness of God."*[81]

True grasp or comprehension of love that actually surpasses knowledge (as most true love does) excludes those who stubbornly cling solely to human intellect as a means of understanding God. *"The power of this love alone enables us to know Christ's immeasurable love."*[82] Because of the cross, God's pain and God's love are too closely interconnected for us or any power to separate. One could stand at the foot of the cross and, relying solely upon human intellect, could logically proclaim God as dead. But one who experiences that crucifixion as the power of God's love for us will know God has never been more alive. Thus, that pain conveys the love that reaches out to embrace the pain of all who are the object of that love.

I don't think we can in fact intellectualize our own pain and suffering which in and of itself has no real or intellectual meaning apart from God. We can understand the workings of the central nervous system and know pain is a mere biological safeguard. That will do nicely until our hurt settles into our bones and then permeates our minds and our hearts. We then know through that experience far more than our minds previously revealed. Only then do we understand pain. It is a bit like the dentist saying, "There will be a little discomfort now" as she is preparing to give us an injection of Novocain in the roof of our mouth. We know that in a few brief moments the Novocain will make the pain tolerable, but neither the dentist's words nor even the drug itself will aid in understanding the pain of the injection. We will understand it only as we experience it. And even then, we will want to put it out of our mind and understanding as quick as possible.

Kitamori's theology is not a thinly disguised masochistic call to celebrate human pain. Rather, it is a means of understanding God's love even in the midst of pain. In our Book of Common Prayer, we have a prayer "For the Sanctification of Illness." It is a prayer I had never previously understood or even used. It reads: "*Sanctify, O Lord, the sickness of your servant (name), that the sense of his weakness may add strength to his faith and seriousness to his repentance; and grant that he may live with you in everlasting life, through Jesus Christ our Lord. Amen.*"[83] Sanctify commonly means to set aside for a purpose and make holy. The superficial notion of making sacred and pure a bodily illness or injury seemed almost a sacrilege. In fact, apart from God's suffering and pain, the mere concept would be profane. Holy

Scripture persists in teaching us to seek and maintain our health and sound minds and bodies.

Like it or not, illness, suffering, and even biological death are part of our earthly journey. Not even Christ chose to avoid the pain in order to be raptured up from an ideal healthy, pain-free human condition. According to John, Christ said, *"Very truly, I tell you, you will weep and mourn, but the world will rejoice; you will have pain, but your pain will turn into joy. When a woman is in labor, she has pain, because her hour has come. But when her child is born, she no longer remembers the anguish because of the joy of having brought a human being into the world. So you have pain now; but I will see you again, and your hearts will rejoice, and no one will take your joy from you."*[84] We will weep, and we will mourn. We will all have pain, and we will all suffer. That's life, that's our inevitable journey. Still, joy is to be ours.

Not because God inflicts pain upon us, but because of God's suffering it is all together fitting that our pain be consecrated and set aside for God's holy purpose. I don't believe God punishes us with pain, but when life brings pain, and it surely will, it can be consecrated to God's purpose. We can, in the great hope of joy, take Christ at his words when he said, "I will see you again." As a woman in labor, our pain has sacred spiritual, if not physical, purposes. We can catch a glimpse of the nature of those purposes in that prayer for sanctification of an illness. From the sense of our own weakness, strength may be added to our weak faith and seriousness to our casual repentance, and we are thus granted everlasting life. In Christ, our physical pain and suffering does not lead to a spiritual deterioration and spiritual death. Rather, pain and suffering shared with our creator help enable new life. New spiritual life is birthed in the midst of pain.

Christ told the Pharisee Nicodemus that, "no one can see the Kingdom of God unless he is born again." I don't think childbirth was merely a casual analogy here. Childbirth is first and foremost painful. It is painful for the mother, and it is painful for the child, and because of that pain, the child finds new life. According to the story in Genesis, the pain of childbirth heralds from the very introduction of all human pain brought on by human sin. This, in turn, coincided with the first demonstration of God's wrath, which, according to Kitamori, coincides with the advent of God's own pain. Nicodemus didn't understand, but in all fairness to him, how could he be expected to understand that which Christ's own apostles struggled so desperately to understand?

Christ referred to his own looming crucifixion as he spoke of a spiritual re-birth required of those who sought after eternal life. He was talking to Nicodemus about a crucifixion that had yet to happen. I think it is easy for us to look back now from our vantage point and see what Nicodemus initially didn't see. Christ was talking about his own crucifixion when he said, *"Just as Moses lifted up the snake in the desert, so the Son of Man must be lifted up, that everyone who believes in him may have eternal life."*[85] So when he mentioned being lifted up, he was referencing God, but maybe not God of the lifted up and glorious heavens; perhaps God as high and lifted up as a Roman Cross. For us contemporary Christians, this is no new image, but for Nicodemus, this was completely new and very radical indeed.

Christ is talking about the cross, and that means pain and death. So what does that dreadful symbol of pain, that instrument of death and torture, have to do with new birth? Pain and suffering are the obvious link. But initially, it seems he is dealing in complete opposites. How could Christ depict the cross as a spiritual birthing station? Everyone knew that cross as a cruel instrument of death.

A view of the cross as a spiritual birthing station is really no more unorthodox than the very core essence of our Christian faith. Through faith, we sinners not only find God's love in the midst of pain, we find new life in the very face of death. The concept is no more of a stretch than Moses' bronze serpent snatching life from the literal jaws of death. It is as proper as the lines from our baptism Rite, "All who are baptized into the death of Jesus Christ may live in the power of his resurrection." All who share in the pain of God will know God's love. I believe those who suffer the disease of cancer can, through their pain, receive a deep insight into the suffering of Christ on the cross, which can lead to new spiritual birth.

Been There – Done That

Once again, the doctor scheduled my second surgery for a date falling within two weeks of our first office appointment, and the ensuing time seemed to fly. I now realize I approached this surgery and recovery with too much of a cavalier attitude. I was over confident as I thought I knew the drill. I prayed a lot, and I expected a smooth ride. I expected my body to react much as it had after the first surgery. In fact, and in spite of, the pre-surgery biopsy, I half way expected the doctor to once again tell me it was all benign. However, not even four months had passed since my body had experienced the trauma of major abdominal surgery. I was to discover that a residual weakness lingered from the first operation even though I felt great and fully recovered. Such invasive surgery presents the body with long-lasting trauma. Still, my only priority was to get in and remove the cancer that was growing within. I just wanted to put it all behind me quickly.

Again, the actual surgery was easy for me; I was out of it and had no sense of just what all my body was enduring. The operation consumed more than seven hours rather than the three hours originally expected. The surgeon found the cancerous portion of the colon entangled with a severely cirrhotic liver. The previous removal of the right kidney had left a cavity, and the cancerous colon had unexpectedly moved into that locale. That surprise greatly slowed the procedure. I had gone into the surgery focused on the surgical procedure and just assumed the recovery process would be a nice, neat, steady progression of daily improvement just as with the first surgery. Such was not to be the case this time with the cirrhosis presenting a real cause of concern.

I had no idea I suffered from cirrhosis of the liver. For many years following blood tests, I had been told that my liver count was borderline low but not so bad as to be a cause for concern. I have never experienced any symptoms that indicated an ailing liver. However, my younger brother Steven had long suffered from 'NAFLD" or Non-alcoholic Fatty Liver Disease. I always mentioned this to the doctors, but absent of any symptoms, no further tests were thought necessary. Thus, the surgeon was left to deal with a low platelet count, one kidney, a cirrhotic liver, and a cancerous colon. My surgeon was up to the task and did a stellar job of balancing all of these unforeseen challenges and still performed a very successful operation. In the final synopsis, an early "stage 2" cancer encapsulated in the small tumor was successfully removed, and there would be no need for chemo-therapy or radiation treatment. This was indeed a good thing as my liver would probably not tolerate either very well.

I was promptly moved from the recovery room to a standard surgical ward but soon experienced extreme dehydration and a racing pulse. So off I went for my first visit to intensive care where they immediately gave me three units of whole blood. I had experienced many types of IV drips before, but this was a remarkable and moving occasion to lie there flat on my back and watch someone else's blood drip into my body. I was being fed intravenously and so my mind raced to capture all of the feelings and overtones of communion. I was overwhelmed with the beauty of that life-sustaining blood entering my body. In truth, I still have far greater emotional and spiritual feelings about that specific experience than I can even today articulate or put in plain words Someday perhaps, I will be able to grasp the full physical, mental, and spiritual connotation of that experience, but for now, suffice it to say that I wondered who had given the blood and was thankful for blood donors. I hope they realize the real value of their gift. In my case, it was the gift of continued life.

> *The dripping blood our only drink,*
> *The bloody flesh our only food:*
> *In spite of which we like to think*
> *That we are sound, substantial flesh and blood –*
> *Again, in spite of that, we call this Friday good.*
> *T.S. Eliot* [86]

Intensive Care was somewhat disconcerting for me as I recalled my clergy visits to ICU almost always warranted administration of the last rites. I had no accurate gauge of my own prognosis. Others always told me how great I was doing even when I wasn't doing so great. I surmised they simply wanted to encourage me. Thus, I was unsure if my condition would improve or grow worse. I prayed and the impact of the whole blood almost immediately made me feel much better and much stronger. My fears soon subsided, and I became comfortable even in Intensive Care.

My family was, of course, there to visit and pray and commented on how much better I looked following the blood transfusion. However, my ICU stay was highlighted by the separate visits of two women whom I have long known and greatly respect. I have considered them both valued spiritual advisors, and yet they approach God in radically different worship modes. Their prayers presented me with an extreme contrast of faith traditions. Both approaches were rich in love, grace, and faith. These extreme spiritual contrasts seemed to comfort and reassure me. It seemed as though I had all my prayer bases covered. These two very different approaches complimented one another and certainly appealed to my ecumenical bent.

The Rev. Nancy Baxter came to visit and pray. She is the Episcopal Chaplain at Emory University and had served as part of a two-person supervisory team for my seminary studies there. As such, she was a person in authority over me with much say about the success of my ordination process. I grew up with two little sisters, and I had a big brother, but I had never experienced the significance of having a big sister. While younger than I, I think the Rev. Baxter in her supervisory role became my academic and even spiritual big sister. Nancy's unique supervisory gift exudes constructive criticism. Never hesitant to point out a weakness or a performance problem, she always did so with respect and drew the seminarian into formulating the remedy. She could provide more leadership and guidance with a simple, gentle question than most managers can do with several demands. I greatly respected that attribute. We seminarians somehow knew that Chaplain Baxter wanted us to succeed in our journey toward ordination; she simply wanted us to do so well equipped for the demands of that call.

Chaplain Baxter came to the Intensive Care Unit to pray with me for healing. She relied heavily upon the Psalms and our Book of Common Prayer. She gently and articulately read ancient words that had been used for centuries, words that simply cannot be improved upon. Her prayers had long been used by others, but they were no less sincere and personal for that point in time in her ministry and my need for healing. Her prayers and readings were powerful, graceful, and faith enhancing.

An hour or two after Nancy departed, Mother Eloise Russell came to visit and pray. Mother Russell is a lay minister with 'The Church of God in Christ', a large Pentecostal denomination. Mother Russell and I shared an office and worked together for years as chaplains at the Atlanta City

Detention Center (the city's adult jail). Mother primarily served the women's inmate population as I provided chaplain services for the male population. There are few people I respect any more than Mother Russell. She is a person of remarkable faith and probably one of the wisest persons I have ever known. Her wisdom comes from an articulate mind, a spiritual gift of discernment, and years of experience. She has experienced pain, suffering, and oppression as few in my generation have known, and yet she exudes great joy and is at peace with her God and her neighbors. Her sense of humor is contagious.

I had long sensed that Mother Russell traveled with a large entourage of unseen angels, and such was the case when she entered my ICU room. I could feel the room change to accommodate a presence that far exceeded the person of Eloise Russell, and that was before she began to pray. I don't believe Mother Russell has ever used a future tense phrase to tell someone she would be praying for them. If someone needs prayer, she prays for them then and there; it matters not if she is on the telephone, in a car, or walking down the sidewalk. She prays extemporaneously, extensively, and out loud. She talks to God, and she listens to God. While I do love the beauty and strength of my prayer book, I must confess that when I am anxious, fearful, and hurting, Mother Russell's approach is most welcome and reassuring. God was there in that room to hear Mother Russell's intercessory prayers.

Blood and prayer; all things considered, that's not bad therapy for any apprehensive believer confined to ICU. Both brought strength and nurture, both brought life. The three packets of blood doubtlessly came from very different persons. Perhaps they came from donors of different ages, races, genders, faiths, cultures, and life styles. But none of that individual disparity mattered in the least as the blood dripped into my bloodstream and there served its common consecrated purpose. Like the blood, all of the prayers offered on my behalf came from very different persons. Like the blood, the individual disparity mattered not to God as sincere intercessory words of faith winged their way into God's heart. I am only left to question why we have allowed petty doctrinal, cultural, and traditional disparity to have such a profoundly divisive effect upon the extended body of Christ on earth.

Within twenty-four hours, I was released from ICU, and another seven days then slowly passed prior to my discharge from the hospital. I was in the hospital for Thanksgiving and celebrated my first semi-solid food which was a pumpkin flavored pudding. I washed it down with a glass of apple juice and still consider it one of the best Thanksgiving Day dinners I have ever enjoyed. My family sat and watched with some sympathy and much amazement over my delight in that small bowl of pudding. Then they were off to the home of great friends who had invited them for the real thing. I was thankful for the pudding and even more thankful for friends who would care enough for my family to include them in their family on that very special day. It may be more blessed to give than to receive, but sometimes it is very blessed to receive.

The following Saturday, I was released and happily went home weak, swollen, and sore. I think the greatest moment with any hospital stay has to be when the nurse removes the final IV tube. That is a sure and certain sign one is actually going home. Needless to say, I felt every bump and pothole along the way home; speed-bumps, even taken at slow speeds, are post-surgical nightmares. When I complained, Judy simply smiled and told me it was finally payback time for the two trips she had endured when I drove her to the hospital just prior to the births of our children. Back then, she accused me of purposefully taking the roughest route to the hospital and hitting every pot-hole along the way. I guess I was in a hurry. Judy's intended humorous response caused me to question just what had happened to the teaching that women would forget the anguish and suffering of childbirth amid all of the joy of bringing a baby into the world. Perhaps there are some momentary exceptions experienced even when those babies are in their thirties.

Once home, I grew quite comfortable as my recovery seemed to be steadily progressing just as hoped for and expected. A week later, I was in the doctor's office for my first post-surgical check, and I was doing so well the doctor cleared me to travel to California so I could be with Judy during the remainder of my recuperation. The journey was relatively uneventful if not comfortable. At six foot four inches tall, I must confess that I have never experienced a comfortable commercial flight this side of First Class. Sitting for hours with one's knees under one's chin is rough enough without the abdominal stitches and staples. So we broke the budget, and I flew first class while my loving spouse suffered in coach. That was tolerable for me at least until we arrived in Salt Lake City where we boarded what is commonly referred to as a 'puddle-jumper' for the final one and a half hour flight into Fresno. That small plane had no first class so we both suffered. I will always be convinced coach class airline seating is designed and configured by very short design engineers.

Silent Night, Holy Night
- Room 513

Once in Fresno, Judy returned to work, and I remained at home during the day, fully expecting to promptly return to this writing. Instead, I remained in bed most of the first few days, grew increasingly lethargic, and lost my appetite. Then in about a week's time, I developed a fever and my abdomen became swollen and greatly distended. Touching it was like touching a granite counter top. So off we went to the nearest emergency room, not knowing a single doctor. I spent my obligatory several hours seated in the very uncomfortable waiting room, and it was during that miserable time we both began to realize just how foolish we had been. I should have remained in Atlanta with my doctors, or we should have contacted and retained local Fresno specialists weeks in advance of our arrival. I guess it was just that we were expecting this recovery to be as smooth as that first post operative experience. Such was not to be the case.

There was one gastro-intestinal surgeon on duty at the hospital, and he was the only doctor available to us. He immediately called for x-rays and then performed a detailed physical examination. He patiently explained that my condition presented all of the indications of a bowel obstruction and said he would have to do immediate exploratory surgery. Neither Judy nor I wanted to hear such a diagnosis as my Atlanta doctors had strongly cautioned us to avoid additional surgery. A third major abdominal incision might possibly be more than I could tolerate. But the Fresno Doctor was insistent that waiting would be extremely dangerous and added that I could wait until it was too late to take corrective action. I didn't like that option, so we reluctantly agreed to proceed with my third major abdominal surgery within five months. It subsequently proved to be a good decision, and we had once again found a good doctor. Prior to the surgery, the doctor reassured Judy by telling her not to worry and added that he never goes into surgery without God. That doctor and God made a pretty good team.

The doctor departed to prepare as two nurses entered my room, carrying some equipment and materials to include three feet of sterile plastic or rubber tubing. They informed me they needed to suction the contents of my stomach, and they were going to insert the tube down through my nose and into the back of my throat. Then I would have to swallow repeatedly as they pushed it down to my stomach. I told them I couldn't do that as I had a terrible gag reflex. The very thought of swallowing that tube made me want to gag. They assured me I wouldn't gag and urged me to just try. I did, and they slowly worked with me until they got it down and into proper position. After about five or ten minutes, I didn't even notice it. During the next eight days, it remained in place relatively ignored.

Now, I won't pretend swallowing that tube was a lot of fun. It was not, and I hope never to have to do that again. I'll take a nice thick steak any day. But I do want to emphasize that none of the procedures performed on me while I was conscious were intolerable or as awful as they sounded. Initially, fear was always my single greatest problem. I was more frightened by what the doctors and nurses would do to me than I was of the disease I was suffering. But I quickly learned that all of those unpleasant procedures brought relief from that illness, and it was the illness that was causing me the real misery.

The surgeon reopened the fresh scar that ran from just below my breast bone

down to below my navel. This was the third time my abdomen had been cut open in five months. The doctor found no bowel obstruction but did find a massive infection of peritonitis spread throughout the abdominal cavity. He cleaned and drained and applied anti-bacteria medicine and closed up the incision. He left two drains in place to continue the removal of infected fluids. Heavy anti-biotic treatment was then initiated.

I did reasonably well during the surgery, but shortly following my arrival in the surgical recovery room, I developed difficulty breathing. Thus, I was once again moved to intensive care where they attached a respirator to do my breathing for me. I started to fight that life-giving respirator, so they put me into a drug-induced coma that was to last four days. Naturally, I have no recall of that time although Judy maintains I did respond to conversation at times. I'll take her word for it; I don't remember a thing. I woke up four days later thinking I had dozed off for an hour or two. Soon, I was back in a general surgical recovery ward for a total stay of fifteen days. That carried me through Christmas.

Dan and Kathy had a small live Christmas tree delivered, and it was strategically placed in the window beside my bed. It survived as I did and is now thriving on my sister's place in the Sierra foothills. I suspect it enjoys being out of the hospital as much as I do. That little tree added just the right touch as my family gathered around my bed for a Christmas Eve gift exchange. We all tried to act like we were having a great time of celebration, and I guess in one sense, we succeeded. We were there solely because we loved one another, and, of course, God's incarnation surfaced amid such family love.

Soon it grew late and my family departed, leaving me alone late Christmas Eve and early Christmas Morn. I was weary, and I thought it would be nice to fall asleep listening to the sound of Christmas carols. I turned on the television and quickly surfed through the many channels and could find no Christmas music. There were Christmas Eve church services with an occasional carol, but all too quickly the delightful music was replaced by the drone of preachers carrying on about the evils of our over-commercialized holiday season. Other channels were featuring infomercials, and then there was an over-abundance of pre-recorded televangelists asking for money so they could continue to finance their broadcast ministry which consisted of "asking for more money." In due course, I settled on a documentary depicting the life and ministry of Billy Graham and dozed off to the background sounds of "Just as I Am" rather than "Silent Night." Merry Christmas to all and to all a good night.

Time passed, and I was home in time for New Year's Eve. Early that day, my doctor came by my room to check on me and told me I was doing much better and might be able to go home in a few days. His visit was almost immediately followed by the hospital's Discharge Coordinator who told me I was being discharged that afternoon because my health insurance company said I had spent enough time in the hospital. Nothing could have made me happier than to go home, but I knew I was too sick to do so. Judy called the doctor who intervened on my behalf, but to no avail. My wife and I had paid our health care premiums for years and years prior to that time. They were paid up in full. But the insurance company, over the objections of my doctor, said I had spent enough time in the hospital. I was free to stay but would have to pay my own expenses as of midnight. Of course, the priest of an inner city mission couldn't possibly afford the thousands of dollars that such would entail. That's why I had the insurance coverage. But the insurance company was not interested in fairness, so I went home sick. I have since tried in vain to identify an analogy for the health care insurance industry within the Ichabod story, but can't find a parallel that callous or evil.

I have long been strongly opposed to socialized medicine and remain so today. However, the lack of compassion and the prevalence of the greed of the health care insurance industry serves to make that very unattractive option appear to me to be the lesser of two evils. I would much prefer government bureaucrats to have no say in my health care. But then I can't imagine they could possibly have greater callous disregard for my personal well-being than the insurance officials I dealt with in my recovery.

So on New Year's Day, I went home prematurely, determined to make the best of a scary and dangerous situation. That evening, I made a New Year's resolution to stay out of hospitals during the coming year. That resolution stood for about four days until once again, I started to swell, hurt, and run a high fever. So it was back into the hospital for another fourteen days. I was readmitted under life-or-death circumstances; again, I was in serious trouble with rampant infection. I should have never been sent home over my doctor's objections. Upon re-admittance, they immediately gave me another CT Scan which revealed a large abscess or concentration of infection just under my liver on my right side. They once again started me on massive doses of antibiotics and went through my side with a long needle to insert a drainage tube and exterior collection bag. I know this procedure sounds terrible, but it was a lot less painful than it sounds.

Fighting a post surgical infection can be very dangerous, but I found it far more frustrating and discouraging than painful. With normal surgical recovery, it seemed every day was a little better than the day before. But with infection, it was quite different. It seemed that just as I started to feel better, I would crash and find myself back in trouble again. Two days after they placed the drain in my right side, I was feeling much better and thinking about going home when my left side started to swell. So it was back for another CT Scan that revealed yet another large abscess in my left side. This, of course, resulted in another drain insertion and yet another disgustingly unsightly collection bag.

This discouraging "good day/bad day" routine started to play havoc with my prayer life. Too often I claimed healing too quickly. Friends would call to see how I was doing, and I would tell them I was doing great and was well on the road to recovery. They would then call back in a day or two and once again they would find me very sick. I guess I let my discouragement begin to show for it was then that I found some dear friends in the faith would not let me be honest. I started to hear comments like, "Don't give up on God," "Keep the faith, He will prevail," and "Hang in there, God is not finished with you yet."

It sounded to me as though those folks thought my faith was far more fragile and tenuous than it was. In reality, my discouragement had nothing to do with my faith. But they seemed to equate my discouragement with a lack of faith in God. I tried to explain to them that a person could be discouraged or frustrated and still have strong faith. Some either couldn't understand that or didn't want to understand it. As with fear, some have great difficulty separating the purely emotional from the spiritual. Fear, frustration, anger, and such are not always programmed signs of spiritual weakness. Friends who are caught in the midst of suffering must be afforded the spiritual freedom to experience human emotion without their faith being impugned by our self-righteous little self-serving clichés. The disease can rob us of much physical and emotional freedom. We need our friends to be there for us, but they should resist the urge to take command of our faith. That is one freedom we need not and dare not surrender to the disease or the control of others.

During his earthly ministry, I believe Christ repeatedly forced a classic confrontation between legalism and God's loving grace. He championed spiritual freedom above cultural and legalistic power. He championed unconditional love above all else. Regardless of the clarity of his teachings in these matters, conflict over these same issues may arise between friends in the faith as one reacts to the other's suffering. I think such conflicts may become more apparent to the sufferer as the suffering drags on in time. Time coalesced with suffering exposes those who would like to spiritually control others. The sufferer's greatest critics are those friends who don't know how to wait on God. Their faith seems to be threatened by God's timing and the sufferer's endurance. Waiting upon God seems to fly in the face of televangelical "Name it and claim it faith." Such critics may be expected to attempt to legalistically justify their own faith by alleging weaknesses in the sufferer's faith and freedom. There are those who will want to define your faith for you. There are those who will be glad to take charge of your faith and your suffering. Don't let them. That job belongs to the Holy Spirit.

In Mark's Gospel, some of the Pharisees and scribes were complaining about Christ's followers failing to wash their hands. He called those Pharisees hypocrites. He quoted the prophet Isaiah who spoke on behalf of God when he said: *"This people honor me with their words, but their hearts are far from me. They teach human precepts* (manmade principles, rules and regulations, petty guidelines and laws) *as doctrines. Thus their worship is in vain"*

French playwright Jacques Deval wrote, *"God loved the birds and invented trees, man loved the birds and invented cages."*[87] In that wonderful quote, I believe Deval captures the difference between the Love of the creator for the created and, all-too-often, the love of the created for one another. The creator loves the created with an unconditional love, as shown by the fact that he is willing to die for those who openly flaunt his law, or as St. Paul words it, "his perfect law, the law of liberty, the law of freedom." Humankind can choose to love one another as God loves but all too often uses the guise of love as a means of control and power over others. In our extended suffering, we may become vulnerable to this control as others seek to build cages for us when they ought to be inventing trees.

The Bible speaks consistently of God's love for us. In the fifth chapter of Paul's letter to the church at Galatia, Paul relates our faith in Christ to our love for him and for one another. In that letter, Paul rejects legalism. He rejects all the rules, the dos and the don'ts in favor of faith. To Paul, the only thing that counts is faith. *"For in Christ Jesus neither circumcision nor uncircumcision count for anything; the only thing that counts is faith working through love."*[88]

"Faith working through love." God loves us, and we love God; we have faith in God, and so we naturally and very sincerely want to please God by doing what is right for our relationship with God (The law of freedom). Sincere love does not need conditions to control behavior. When we love God and one another, we don't need people who think they are God, running around setting up petty rules for us to follow. Because of Christ, we no longer follow the Ten Commandments because they are the law and because we have been ordered to obey them. Now, we strive to obey those commandments because we love God in return, and thus, we just naturally want to please God. That's faith working through unconditional love. We don't attend church because it's some kind of church rule that we have to be there every Sunday. We attend because we love God and because we love to be with others who share that love and faith, and we love to worship a God that is love.

Christ counsels us to love God, love neighbor, and love self. When we sin, we know we hurt God, our neighbors, and ourselves. We betray God, we betray our neighbors, and we betray ourselves. We repent of our sin, not because we are afraid of going to hell for breaking the rules. We repent because Jesus loves us enough to die for us and because we regret betraying His trust and his love.

Still, there are folks who just don't get it. They are afraid of freedom. They think unconditional love must surely be a license for others to sin at will. And like the Pharisees, they are not going to tolerate it. They don't trust us with the freedom God gives us, so they make, monitor, enforce, and ultimately judge our behavior against their man-made rules. They often claim for scripture what scripture does not claim for itself. Consequently, they will love and accept us only if our hands are clean and compliant with a thousand other little contrived rules and regulations. Ultimately, they are in charge rather than God, and all shamelessly in the name of a God who is love.

It is interesting to note that if Christ would have continued in that quote from Isaiah, he would have told those Pharisees, "*You turn things upside down! Shall the potter be regarded as the clay? Shall things made, say of its maker, He did not make me; or things formed say of the one who formed it, "He has no understanding." Then the meek shall obtain fresh joy in the Lord for the tyrant shall be no more.*"[89] God wants us to behave ourselves. He wants us to choose to do so out of love, not out of fear or in compliance to enforceable rules and regulations. Again, God makes trees – not cages!

Perhaps those who suffer cherish spiritual freedom more than others because the disease itself is so controlling. Paul suffered a lot and, of course, wrote a lot about spiritual freedom. The one who is struggling with pain does not need some self-appointed Sunday School tyrant challenging him or her in a tedious game of moral ping pong. Such pious one-up-man-ship will lead only to additional frustration and discouragement.

In the midst of all my discouragement and frustration, I started to grow very weary and longed to rest in peace. Those words have been so over-used and abused that they have lost their power and their true meaning and beauty for many of us. But a little suffering and a lot of discouragement can spiritually and emotionally wear a person out, and the thought of resting in God's arms can become very attractive. As such, a person comes to better understand some of St. Paul's more radical writing about life and death. *"We would rather be away from these earthly bodies, for then we would be at home with the Lord."* Paul must have been quite weary when he wrote those words. This was something that I could not understand prior to my own experience with being so very weary and discouraged. One night, I did pray, asking God to hurry up and come get me. I was extremely discouraged, but my faith was never stronger. You know it had to be strong for me to sincerely pray that prayer. By the way, I awoke the next morning and hastily thanked God for ignoring that prayer. It hadn't taken long for me to change my mind; I no longer wanted to die. Of course, God did answer that prayer.

The Visitor

Toward the end of this hospital stay, I experienced something that I must write about. It had been a troubled, frustrating, and difficult previous day caused not by pain but from the discouragement of continuing relapses. In fact, with the additional new drain and massive doses of antibiotic medicine came renewal of strength and a real sense that the infection was starting to wane. But I had been there before only to experience relapse and pessimistically expected the same from this surge of energy and health. I couldn't sleep and tossed and turned as much as one could with plastic tubes coming out just under the rib cage of both sides. Soon, it was midnight and the new beginning of January 15th. I had been in the hospital for a total of thirty-eight days since my surgery of November 18th. Soon, it was four A.M., and the nurses entered to flush my drains and turned out all the lights as they exited the room. Then there, in the darkness, a very unexpected, never-before-experienced, and remarkable spiritual happening occurred. If it weren't so real to me, I would merely dismiss it as wishful imagination. But it was every bit as real as reality itself, and it left me with a relevant and crucial message that did not originate in my mind or spirit.

Once written down, the account of this incident may become problematic for some readers. Accounts of the supernatural almost always force the reader into an immediate hard choice between total skepticism or complete compliance and subjugation of thought. I am aware of this and concerned about it for I am not writing this exclusively for those who share my particular faith and fervor. I do so disdain "in-your-face" Christian witness. Yes, it worked for Christ at times, but I am not Christ. I strive to be more like Him, but I have a long way to go before I can walk into someone else's temple with a whip over-turning tables and running out the evil money-changers. In the meantime, I can work on replicating His more prevalent gentleness, humility, and love.

Thus, I encourage the reader to interpret this account as she or he chooses. You may chalk it up to an over-active imagination spurred on by mild sleep-deprivation, normal dreaming, hallucinations or delusions, mesmerization, or even self hypnosis. Or you are free to agree with my conclusion that it was Christ's Holy Spirit present with me in an unusually pertinent sense. Again, I don't need to know how God does something; He has so many resources at His command. The truly important issue is that I recognize God and receive that which He presents as truth. It is important that I then check that truth against the truth of Holy Scripture. In this writing, it is my simple hope that the reader will receive this account in the spirit of freedom of thought and introspection.

It was 4 A.M., and surprisingly, the darkness brought comfort and peace to my troubled night. I could see the city lights out my window below, and I felt snug there in that hospital bed. I was off all narcotics by then and was taking only an occasional Tylenol as needed, thus I was pain free. This comfortable, dark, quiet, solitary moment seemed like the opportune time to pray. So I started to pray extemporaneously, "God, thank you for this sense of recovery and the renewal of strength. I don't know why you let me suffer so much for so long..." This brief prayer opener was immediately interrupted by something that silenced me for the moment.

My eyes were closed, but the eyes of my heart were startled by the sight of a young man sitting on the side of my bed. He spoke immediately to the words of my brief prayer opener. My physical eyes were closed, but my ears were wide open, and I immediately recognized the voice of my Shepherd; I recognized the voice of Christ or his Holy Spirit. Without that clear comforting audible voice, I may not have known Him. It was the first time I had heard an audible voice from God, but it seemed so familiar and loving. My heart's-eye view of Him remained true to St. Paul's standard of seeing through a glass darkly. I could not determine facial features. What I saw was very consistent with the conjured mental image of Christ I have long carried which has obviously been derived from viewing Christian art. I saw the blurred image of a young, medium dark-skinned man with a beard and dark, shoulder-length hair. His posture was relaxed, and he wore a dusty, natural sackcloth robe.

My brief interrupted prayer opener was, "I don't understand why I had to suffer so." Christ's immediate audible answer was, "You were such a tough one to break. I love you very much, and you have loved me all your life, but you are supposed to be growing and changing in my spirit. You have always thought of yourself first, and that obstructs your love and spiritual growth. I had to get your attention, you must think of me first if you are to grow and mature in me."

Foolishly, I was more taken with the reality of the encounter rather than the sobering content of the message. This was actually happening! I can remember thinking, "This may be my only opportunity to get a clear answer to my primary question." I asked, "So, where do I go from here? What should my ministry be? Where should it be? What is your plan for the rest of my life? What should I do?" I then confidently waited for an answer to my questions. My answer came in the form of what seemed like a loving but very exasperated sigh.

Then followed loving, patient words, "That is exactly
what I am talking about! Your ministry, your life, is all about
you, not me. You are doing my work, but you are your own
first priority. It is my work you are doing. I should be your
first priority."

The Spirit of Christ continued, "OK, let's try this. For
right now, you are nothing." That caught my attention as I
realized its truth and was surprised by a feeling of relief and
love. "You are not a husband, you are not a father, and you
are not an ordained priest. You have no long line of good
friends just lined up to wish you well. You have no ministry,
you have no church, no flock, you have no responsibility,
and you have no respect or prestige. You have no home, and
you have no material possessions. You have nothing and you
are nothing, except you are still my friend. **Is that sufficient
for you?**"

I started to cry as I experienced the lifting of my heavy
burden which was nothing more than my own weight. I was
trying to carry myself while God wanted to carry me. I had
been doing God's work as part of my self-pious resume. I
was narcissistically my own first priority, thus I was my own
heaviest burden. Peace and Christ's love settled deep into
my soul as I realized and answered that all I really needed
was Christ. I never felt the love of Christ as strongly as at
that moment, and I never felt my love for him so intensely
focused. That love is more than sufficient. His grace is
more than sufficient. In fact, in biological death, I will have
nothing and be nothing except Christ's love. That is very
sufficient indeed.

That gentle and loving voice then continued to address
the little self-pity party I had been enjoying prior to this holy
visit. He assured me that I had endured nothing more and a
lot less than a good many other faithful folk. He diminished
the discomfort of my side drains by contrasting them with
the wound left by a crude Roman spear, and then the vision

and audible voice were gone, but the spirit remained. Paul's words echoed back once again, "*I pray that, according to the riches of his glory, he may grant that you may be strengthened in your inner being with power through his spirit, and that Christ may dwell in your hearts through faith, as you are being rooted and grounded in love.*"[90] I then cried myself to sleep with tears of great joy and peace.

I slept sound and late the next morning which was a Sunday. One of my more regular nurses entered the room and surprised me with a question. She asked, "You don't have anything to do with the Episcopal Church do you?" I hesitated as I recalled the gentle voice, "You have nothing and you are nothing, except you are still my friend." I realized that truth but knew it was not the correct answer to the nurse's morning-after question. I simply answered, "Yes, I am an Episcopal Priest." The nurse was surprised, and I humorously pondered what that was all about. What had I done to make that seem so implausible?

Immediately, a couple of strangers entered my room carrying a vase of beautiful cut flowers. The wife spoke, "Father Moline, we are from St. Columba's, and we brought you flowers from this morning's altar." They presented the flowers, and in that moment, they were no longer strangers; they were my brother and sister. They called me Father, and I realized I was still a priest after all. They placed the vase of flowers in my window, we had a brief loving chat, I thanked them profusely, and they left not knowing the significant impact their humble flower-ministry had played in the spiritual renewal of my ordination vows.

Soon, Judy entered my room, and she acted as though she was still my wife of thirty-nine years. Later that afternoon, my daughter called, and with her usual cheerful voice, she said, "Hi dad, this is Becca." I realized I was still a father. Friends called to check on my recovery, and even the Deacon from Holy Comforter Church called to discuss a church business matter. All came back to me as I pondered my personal and spiritual priorities in all of these relationships. I now understood these riches did not revolve around me, they belonged to Christ. I knew I had to apply Christ's 4 A.M. message to my continued existence in a very practical manner. I was, and am still, not sure just how to go about that. How much of the effort should I leave to the Spirit, and to what extent can I contribute toward maintaining a correct spiritual balance? It appears I will have the opportunity to attempt to live out that message as I was shortly discharged from the hospital, grew in strength, and flew home to Georgia to continue my recovery.

Isaiah returned to tell King Hezekiah that God had seen him crying, heard his faithful plea, and had decided to add fifteen years to his time here on earth. But Ichabod was to have no such term guarantee. We know of his birth and his naming, and then he immediately slipped off the radar screen of Holy Scripture. There is no further mention made of him in the text. He may have lived a few days, or like his grandfather Eli, he may have lived into his nineties. We don't know, and we are left to assume his longevity was not crucial to the message presented in the First Book of Samuel. However, this in no way implies his life was not significant to God.

It is interesting to consider that, if Ichabod survived childhood, he would have been in his early twenties when a victorious King David finally brought the Ark home to Jerusalem. With Eli as his grandfather and Phinehas as his father, it is not inconceivable that he was himself a priest or at least being prepared for the priesthood by the time of that grand celebration. Perhaps Ichabod eventually cared for the Ark and the presence of God among his chosen people. After all, God had promised Eli that his *"family and the family of your ancestors should go in and out before me forever;"*[91] But then God apparently reversed that personal promise and declared to Eli, *"See, a time is coming when I will cut off your strength and the strength of your ancestor's family, so that no one will live to old age.*"[92] It does seem highly unlikely God would have reversed himself a second time with such remaining unrecorded in 1st Samuel. Thus, Ichabod drops from the narrative.

Like Ichabod, Eleazar was to have no such "Hezekiah style" life-term guarantee, either. We know he was ordained to care for the Ark, and then he, too, is never again referred to in scripture. It does seem a bit odd that twenty years later when David came to escort the Ark back to Jerusalem there was no reference to this man who was consecrated to care for the presence of God. His brothers, Uzzah and Ahio, were selected to drive the ox cart carrying the Ark back to Jerusalem. That ill-conceived task was carried out in a manner that was very contrary to God's commandment, and it would ultimately cost Uzzah his life. Perhaps Eleazar recognized the obvious disobedience and resulting danger in such a procedure and refused to participate. On the other hand, perhaps Eleazar had simply died of old age long before David's journey to Kiriath-Jearim. Again, this is really anyone's guess.

We are left to surmise that Eleazar's longevity must have been relatively insignificant. The significance of his life is briefly recorded in scripture, and that significance is to be found in the fact that he was consecrated to proclaim and care for the presence of God among God's people. Like all believers, he was called to answer the Ichabod question while drawing a minimum of attention to his own significance. Where is the glory? Alas, God's glory is not to be found solely in our healthy longevity. God's glory is to be found in Christ's death at a young age following only three years of known active ministry. God's glory is to be found at Golgotha. "Where is the Glory?" God's Glory is to be found in God's pain. "Where is the Glory?" God's Glory is to be found in God's love.

The Leaning Tree

⌒

I grew up in the central San Joaquin Valley in California and returned to spend most of my post-surgical recuperation there with Judy. By the seventh week following my first surgery, I had started to drive again and had regained much of my strength and stamina. So while Judy was at work one day, I left Talbot at home and drove by myself east-bound up highway #180 to 7,000 feet elevation and the Sequoia-Kings Canyon National Park. There was something up there that I dearly wanted to see and touch. At some unknown time close to the date of my surgery, that is sometime between mid June and the last week in June of 2005, "The Leaning Tree" had toppled over onto the ground, spanning the entire breadth of Lion Meadow.

Once through the gate of the park, I drove several miles to the General Grant Grove and found a parking space in the public lot near the renowned and celebrated General Grant Tree. As with most of California's scenic attractions, that day presented the usual wall-to-wall tourists and sight-seers. At first, I was just one sightseer in the crowd. The teeming hordes jam-packed the self-guiding tour path that leads up the mountain to the General Grant Tree, the Robert E. Lee Tree, the Fallen Monarch (toppled centuries ago), and other high profile attractions. I broke away from the crowd, walked to the far end of the Bus and RV parking lot, and found the unmarked entrance to the lesser traveled "Sunset Trail." A few yards down the path, I found myself pretty much on my own, leaving the crowd, noise, and bustle behind. The "Leaning Tree," informally named by locals from the nearby YMCA camp, had never been a major tourist attraction, and even its fall drew very little attention.

"The Leaning Tree" was relatively small, young, and unimpressive. Although it was a member of the Sequoiadendron Giganteum species and thus a member of the family that comprise the largest living things on earth, this particular tree was known primarily for its defective "lean" which was first noted some fifty years ago. The "Leaning Tree" was not all that tall for a Sequoia; it was only slightly taller than a twenty story building and only about ten centuries old. That's young in sequoia-years. Sequoias don't die of old age and have been known to live in excess of 3,000 years.[93] Most do die as a result of toppling over, and thus the "Leaning Tree" was toppled over in the prime of its life at age 1,000.

I walked Sunset Trail for a little more than one-half mile down the side of the mountain. The trail followed "Big Tree Creek" as it cascaded over fern-covered granite rock formations down to the bottom. The trail then levels out as it skirts "Lion Meadow." I first spotted the huge and peculiar looking thirty-foot tall dirt ball and the massive exposed root system from the trail as I approached the serene meadow. The crater left by the sudden massive upheaval was significant and had started to fill with water. New ferns lined the resulting shaded pool.

That giant did span the delightful little meadow with its crest making its way into the wooded area on the far side. The lesser vegetation of the meadow floor, the grasses, wildflowers, and seedlings were now snuggly embracing the entire length of the fallen giant. My first and lasting impression was that of Michelangelo's "Pieta." I looked at the meadow and saw in nature, in God's own creation, both the beauty and the sorrow of a mother embracing her adult child in death. I reached out and touched the rough skin of the enormous fallen body. In the noonday sun, it was warm and even soft to the touch.

I stood there and considered the miracle of life and how a thousand years earlier in that very same spot, that tree was but a small and vulnerable grass-like blade sprouting from a seed the size of an oatmeal flake. I then reflected upon the words of the 90th Psalm: *"You turn us back to dust and say, go back, O child of earth. For a thousand years in your sight are like yesterday when it is past. You sweep us away like a dream; we fade away suddenly like the grass."* A thousand years are like yesterday, and yet I'm ecstatic over the possibility of another ten to twenty years of this life. I was reminded of just how narrow my vision and how small my thinking is in contrast to God's.

My attention was then drawn to the spiders, ants, and other small critters now making their life there on the fallen body of the tree. They, too, are God's creatures just as surely as the tree, and yet they are organisms with life spans doubtlessly measured in mere weeks if not days rather than centuries. I reflected upon the relativity of time. *"The days of our years are threescore years and ten; and if by reason of strength they be fourscore years, yet is their strength labor and sorrow; for it is soon cut off, and we fly away!"* Then I looked up to the clear, blue California sky and halfway expected to see an eagle soaring up there. But the empty sky reminded me the eagle was not in God's plan for me just yet.

But one of these days, I am going to fly away. Most of us now frequent modern airports too often to get all that excited about flying away. But still, those King James' words are inspirational. I suspect we do lose some of the beauty and inspiration of that 90th Psalm because of our technical and modern way of life. However, back when this psalm was first sung, no one could have even imagined the noise, long lines, and hassles of todays air travel. They did know eagles though, and so I think in a way, this psalm comes echoing down across the ages to confront us with the question, "Can we still focus our lives upon the wings of eagles?" Can we look at our own hour of death and envision an eagle taking to flight?

On the night before my very first surgery, I opened my Book of Common Prayer to the Burial Service, sat down at the word processor, and hammered out my own funeral plans. I named the preacher and celebrant, the readings, the music, and all of the other optional details. These matters are not all that important to me, but like the "Living Will," the "Power of Attorney," and other such post-death business matters, I simply wanted to spare Judy the burden of seemingly endless decision making. Actually, I secretly suspect Judy would enjoy planning what is truly a grand worship service in the Episcopal Church and tradition. I myself regret being unable to attend, but I do know Judy would do a far superior job of selecting the music. None the less, I completed this relatively inconsequential chore by writing out my request to be cremated, but then realized I had no preference as to where my ashes should be spread. I suggested that Judy use her own discretion.

While not my greatest concern, I do now have a preference as to my final resting place. I would like my ashes spread in Lion Meadow. I am certain there are all sorts of bureaucratic federal park prohibitions against such, but I know of no real or lasting or even temporary negative environmental impact that would result. I suspect that having grown up with the local Police Chief as their dad, my adult children probably retain just enough disregard for petty federal bureaucratic authority to make quick work of successfully smuggling my ashes down to the meadow in a common hiker's backpack or some other contrivance of their own genius. Just as surely as my spirit will someday soar away through the skies, my body must return to the dust, and I can think of no lovelier place to return to the elements than there in Lion Meadow on the western slope of the high Sierra Nevadas.

In that 90th Psalm, the beauty of symbolic language embraces the beauty of stark reality much as the beauty of "Lion Meadow" embraces the fallen giant; much as love embraces suffering. It is a beauty we can truly savor and celebrate, and a reality we can squarely face, only because of the reality of another tree. I am referring to a tree that became a bloody Roman cross which must in turn be considered against the real stark beauty of an empty tomb on Easter morning. We can focus our attention upon Good Friday or we can direct our thoughts to Easter Morning, but the truth is Good Friday and Easter cannot be separated any more than we can separate the hope from the despair of the 90th Psalm. We wouldn't have Easter without the crucifixion - and we couldn't bear the crucifixion without Easter. In the midst of life's despair, I choose to rejoice; *"Christ will come again in glory to judge the living and the dead, and his kingdom will have no end." "I look for the resurrection of the dead, and the life of the world to come."*

King Hezekiah closed his poem: *"Each generation tells of your faithfulness to the next. Think of it. The Lord is ready to heal me! I will sing his praises with instruments every day of my life in the Temple of the Lord."*[94] While no king, I have been delivered from death for the same reason Hezekiah was delivered, to sing songs of praise! Of course, my poor singing voice may hamper me somewhat. I can't sing well, but I can preach and teach the gospel. I can celebrate the sacraments. I can pray, praise, counsel, write, and rejoice. I can feed the hungry, clothe the naked, welcome the strangers, and visit those in jail. I can love the unlovely. I can respect the dignity of every human being. I can be a good steward of God's creation and all that he has given me. Like Eleazar, I can celebrate God's presence among God's people. I can be a better rector, husband, father, and friend. I can believe, and

I can put Christ first in my life. I can love God, neighbor, and self. Thus, I can truly look forward with peace of mind and heart to the day I will be delivered by death rather than from death. *"For it is in giving that we receive; it is in pardoning that we are pardoned; and it is in dying that we are born to eternal life. Amen."*[95]

Endnotes

1 NRSV Matthew 16:24
2 American Cancer Society Cancer Facts and Figures 2012 p.1
3 American Cancer Society Cancer Facts and Figures 2012 p.1
4 Kitamori, Kazoh Theology of the Pain of God 5th p.52 Edition John Knox Press 1965
5 NRSV Ecclesiastes 3:1
6 Merton, Thomas No Man is an Island 1955 Harcourt, Inc.
7 NRSV Ezekiel 7:5
8 New Living Translation Isaiah Chapter 38
9 NRSV Romans Chapter 8
10 NRSV Philippians Chapter 4
11 Boswell, James Life of Johnson Barnes and Noble 252
12 NRSV John 14:27
13 NIV Psalm 23
14 NIV Matthew 28:18
15 NRSV Matthew 26:41
16 NIV Psalm 90 V. 12
17 Lewis C.S. Letter to Sheldon Vanauken 4/17/1951
18 NRSV Jeremiah Chapter 6
19 Kosuke Koyama The Crucified Christ Challenges Human Power Asian Faces of Jesus / R.S. Sugitharajah, Editor Orbis 1997
20 The Atlanta Journal-Constitution Oct 4th, 2005 Page #B5

21 NRSV Matthew 12
22 NRSV Luke Chapter 18
23 NRSV Matthew 25
24 NRSV St John 15:15
25 NRSV *Sirach*
26 Merton, Thomas No Man is an Island 1955 Harcourt, Inc.
27 NRSV Psalm 53
28 Harold G. Koenig & Andrew J. Weaver, Counseling Troubled Older Adults 1997 Abingdon Press
29 Nowen, Henri J. M. The Wounded Healer 1979 Doubleday
30 NLT Isaiah
31 Merton, Thomas No Man is an Island 1955 Harcourt, Inc.
32 Book of Common Prayer 1892
33 NRSV Luke 23:43
34 NRSV John Chapter 12
35 NRSV John Chapter 12
36 Merton, Thomas No Man is an Island 1955 Harcourt, Inc.
37 The Book of Common Prayer 1979 An Order for Burial
38 The Book of Common Prayer 1979 Ministration at the Time of Death
39 The Book of Common Prayer 1979 Ministration at the Time of Death
40 The Book of Common Prayer 1979 Ash Wednesday
41 NLT 2 Corinthians 5:6
42 NLT Isaiah 38
43 NIV Isaiah 64
44 NRSV John Chapter 8
45 NRSV Genesis Chapter 1
46 Tillich, Paul "The Eternal Now" 1963 Charles Scribner & Sons NY,NY p.123
47 Tillich, Paul "The Eternal Now" 1963 Charles Scribner

& Sons NY,NY p.123

48 NRSV Psalm 107

49 King James Chapter 16

50 Martin Buber <u>I and Thou</u> Charles Scribner's Sons 1970

51 Lewis, C. S. <u>The Four Loves</u> Harcourt Brace Jovanovich 1960

52 Lewis, C. S. <u>A Grief Observed</u> Bantam 1976

53 Kosuke Koyama, <u>Water Buffalo Theology</u> Orbis Books Maryknoll, NY 1999 p.83

54 Richard A. Norris, <u>Understanding the faith of the Church</u> Harper San Francisco 1979 p.101

55 Kitamori, Kazoh <u>Theology of the Pain of God</u> John Knox Press 1965

56 Kitamori, Kazoh <u>The Theology of the Pain of God</u> John Knox Press 1965 p.60

57 Spong, John <u>A New Christianity for a New World</u> Harper San Francisco 2001

58 Spong, John <u>Here I Stand</u> Harper San Francisco 1999

59 Kerr, Hugh T. <u>Readings in Christian Thought</u> 1966 Abingdon Press

60 Gomes, Peter J. Sermon: "<u>The Mystery of Our Religion</u>" Harper San Francisco 1998

61 Eliot, T.S. Collected Poems 1909-1962 P. 147 'The Rock' Harcourt Brace & World

62 Eliot, T. S. Collected Poems 1909-1962 P.187 'East Coker' Harcourt Brace & World

63 NRSV Hosea Chapter 11:8 & 9

64 Book of Common Prayer <u>Burial of the Dead</u> Rite II

65 NIV Isaiah 38:2

66 NRSV Romans Chapter 5

67 NRSV Job Chapter 1

68 NLT Isaiah Chapter 38

69 Gomes, Peter J. Sermon: "<u>What's in a miracle?</u>" Harper San Francisco 1998

70 NRSV Exodus Chapter 23

71 NLT Exodus 25

72 NRSV Hebrews Chapter 12

73 NRSV Ecclesiastes 7:3

74 NRSV Mark Chapter 8

75 NRSV Hebrews Chapter 2

76 Jones, L. Gregory <u>Embodying Forgiveness</u> Eerdmans 1995

77 Jones, L. Gregory <u>Embodying Forgiveness</u> Eerdmans 1995

78 NRSV John's Gospel Chapter 10

79 Tanakh Psalm 68

80 Kitamori, Kazoh <u>The Theology of the Pain of God</u> John Knox Press 1965 p. 146

81 NRSV Ephesians 3: 16-19

82 Kitamori, Kazoh <u>The Theology of the Pain of God</u> John Knox Press 1965 p. 146

83 The Book of Common Prayer p. 460

84 NRSV John 16: 20-22

85 NIV John 3: 14

86 Eliot, T.S. Collected Poems 1909-1962 P.188 'East Coker' Harcourt Brace & World

87 Rhodes, Barbara K. & Odell, Rice <u>A Dictionary of Environmental Quotes</u> p.22 John Hopkins

88 NRSV Galatians Chapter 5

89 NRSV Isaiah Chapter 29

90 NRSV Ephesian Chapter 3

91 NRSV 1st Samuel Chapter 2

92 NRSV 1st Samuel Chapter 2

93 Engbeck Jr., Joseph H. <u>The Enduring Giants</u> 1988 CA. Dept. of Parks

94 NLT Isaiah 38

95 The Book of Common Prayer p. 833

CPSIA information can be obtained at www.ICGtesting.com
Printed in the USA
BVOW030904170812

298105BV00001B/2/P